CARVING
Cypress
Knees

WRITTEN BY
CAROLE JEAN BOYD

PHOTOGRAPHY BY
JACK A. WILLIAMS

ISBN: 978–1–56523–271–6

Publisher's Cataloging-in-Publication Data

Boyd, Carole Jean.

    Carving cypress knees / written by Carole Jean Boyd ; photography
by Jack A. Williams. -- East Petersburg, PA : Fox Chapel Publishing, c2005.

       p. ; cm.

       ISBN: 1-56523-271-2
       ISBN-13: 978-1-56523-271-6

       1. Woodwork--Patterns. 2. Wood-carving. 3. Wood-carved
figurines. I. Williams, Jack A. II. Title.

TT199.7 .B69 2005
736/.4--dc22   0509

To learn more about the other great books
from Fox Chapel Publishing, or to find a
retailer near you, call toll-free 800-457-9112
or visit us at **www.FoxChapelPublishing.com.**

Note to Authors: We are always looking for talented authors
to write new books in our area of woodworking,
design, and related crafts. Please send a brief letter
describing your idea to Acquisition Editor,
1970 Broad Street, East Petersburg, PA 17520.

Printed in China
First printing: October 2005
Second printing: July 2009

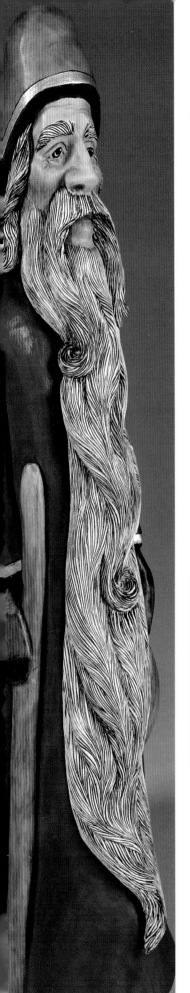

Table of Contents

1

3

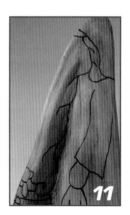
11

21

40

66

82

Carole Jean Boyd

As a young girl of 16, Carole Jean began an apprenticeship to a local photographer. There she learned how to retouch negatives and paint photographs. When black-and-white photography went out of vogue and color was the new thing, she conquered a new medium. She was widely respected in her field and won many national awards through the Professional Photographers of America. Carole Jean traveled all over the Southeast teaching photographic art to labs, studios, and state conventions much like she travels and teaches woodcarving today. She feels that all the years of retouching and painting faces is what shaped her style of carving. Once you've gotten to know her work, it is easily recognizable— an enchanting blend of realism, caricature, and a little primitive, a style that seems to have evolved by itself. She enjoys the challenge of carving cypress knees, though she works in many other kinds of wood.

Carole Jean makes her home in Millbrook, Alabama, and enjoys spending time with her four children and six grandchildren when she's not working or on the road teaching. She has won Best of Show awards at the Blue Earth Show in Minnesota and at the War Eagle Fall Fair in Arkansas. Carole Jean has also received first-place ribbons in numerous competition shows, including the International Woodcarvers Congress, Dollywood Woodcarving Showcase, Wonders in Wood, Southeastern Woodcarvers Competition, Heart of Dixie Woodcarving Show, Mid-South Show, and Artistry in Wood. She has taught at numerous schools, such as John C. Campbell Folk School in Brasstown, North Carolina; Southeastern Woodcarving School in Montgomery, Alabama; War Eagle Seminar in Hindville, Arkansas; Rally on the Rio in Mercedes, Texas; The Woodcarving Retreat in West Greenwich, Rhode Island; and many, many other woodcarving clubs in the U.S.

Carole Jean also enjoys writing articles for *Wood Carving Illustrated* and *Chip Chats* and holds private classes at her Old South Wood Carving Studio in Montgomery, Alabama.

Jack A. Williams

Jack is a retired commercial photographer living in Sun City West, Arizona. Photography was once a hobby for Jack until he discovered he could make a living doing what he enjoyed. He then needed a new hobby, so, in 1973, he started carving wood by carving an eagle plaque from scrap lumber, not knowing that was not a recommended carving wood. Jack continued to carve birds, competing at the Ward World Wildfowl Competition for ten years. His first exposure to caricature carving was a Harold Enlow class in 1988, which had a lasting effect on the direction of his carving. Jack still enjoys studying caricature carving with many great carvers not only to learn new skills but also to fellowship with interesting people and to have a fun time.

His artistic talents have been demonstrated with a third Best of Show in the first CCA National Caricature Carving Competition, a Best of Show at the Ward World Wildfowl Carving Competition, a Best of Show at the Dayton Artistry in Wood Show, People's and Carver's Choice and Best of Wood Sculpture at Dollywood, and Best of Division at the International Woodcarvers Congress. Jack also won first place in the Flexcut Tool Internet Carving Competition in 2001.

October 2004 marked the thirteenth year for him to coordinate the woodcarving show at Dollywood and the second year to coordinate the National Caricature Carving Competition and Exhibit, which was also held at Dollywood. Jack became a member of the Caricature Carvers of America in 2003. He is also a founding member of the Tennessee Carvers Guild. Jack now spends a great deal of time photographing carvings at shows and for friends, and his photography appears frequently in many magazines on woodcarving and other subjects.

Along with Vic Hood, Jack co-authored both *Carving Found Wood* and the most recent book, *Extreme Pumpkin Carving*. Jack and Rick Jensen recently completed a book on carving whimsical bark houses, entitled *Illustrated Guide to Carving Tree Bark*. Fox Chapel publishes all three books.

Jack's carvings are not available for sale. You can write to him at 22205 N. Golf Club Drive, Sun City West, Arizona 85375.

In memory of

Moose and Bryan Lindsey

They recruited me and boosted my confidence all along the way.

I still hear a whisper every now and then.

— Carole Jean

Acknowledgments

This book has been a labor of love and could never have been done
without the help and encouragement of so many people.

First of all, to the instructors that I have studied with, and there have been
many. I thank these four in particular: James Cecil, my first instructor and
constant mentor for many years; John Burke, for teaching me about the
muscles of the face, what they can and cannot do, and how they lie under the
skin; Harold Enlow, for teaching me to have fun, to not take carving so
seriously, and to just enjoy the carving; Janet Cordell for teaching me to
always look at things realistically, whether I carve them that way or not.
Thank you.

To Allen Carmichael for never letting me doubt that
I could do this, thank you.

To Jack Williams, my co-author, your photography is nothing less than
wonderful! You were so kind and patient throughout this whole time.
Thank you.

To Carole Williams, I just don't think I could have done this without
you. You and your computer opened up a whole new world to me.
Thank you for your invaluable photographic editing and all the extra
work caused because I can't type.

Last, but certainly foremost, I thank God for giving me the talent to
carve and the ability to teach.

— Carole Jean

The Enticing World of Cypress Knees

Carole Jean invites anyone who's interested in the history of the South or in carving cypress knees to visit her in Old Alabama Town at the South's premier history village. The Old South Woodcarving Studio is located at 431 Columbus Street, right in the middle of more than 50 authentically restored nineteenth- and twentieth-century structures.

A corner inside Carole Jean's shop, The Old South Woodcarving Studio, is filled with cypress knees in various stages of carving.

My hope as you read this book and then start carving is that you will be as captivated as I am by these strange, wonderful, beautiful, ugly, massive, delicate, silly-looking growths that we call cypress knees. Sitting in a room full of knees trying to decide which one to carve next is a bit like opening a Whitman's Sampler of chocolates and trying to decide which one to enjoy first. They are all so different, and each suggests such a wide variety of things that you can carve.

I carved my first knee in 1990. Once you get one carved, carving cypress knees just kind of takes over your life. They seem to beckon to you. Little whispers of "Come and get me, you know what I am" just dance around in my head. Most of the time, I do know what they are, but sometimes I don't know until they are done.

Now, go pick one out and just see how much fun they are to carve.

Ya'll come,

Carole Jean Boyd

Cypress Trees and Knees

I can't think of anything more majestic—and Southern—than a beautiful cypress swamp. In the daytime, the cypress swamp can look absolutely glorious and full of splendor, but, at night, the moss-draped trees and the knees coming up out of the water can make it look downright spooky.

While cypress swamps are typical of the southern states, they can be found as far north as Delaware and Illinois. In America, we have bald cypress and pond cypress. Both are conifers (evergreen trees) and relatives of the redwood tree. They are wetland trees, though they can occasionally be found outside of that environment.

Bald cypress is the larger of the two types, sometimes growing 150 to 160 feet tall and 6 to 17 feet in diameter and living to be hundreds of years old—with some over a thousand years old. It is truly a giant of a tree. Bald cypress has a thin, tight bark. The sapwood is almost white, and the heartwood can range from light yellow to a beautiful, rich chocolate color. It is sometimes called the "graybeard of the swamp," a name that I think is just wonderful considering what I do with the knees from the tree. Bald cypress grows along riverbanks and swamps, along streams, and along the edges of lakes and spring runs.

Pond cypress is generally smaller than bald cypress, though it sometimes is still quite large. It has a thicker, shaggier bark than its counterpart. In certain locations, pond cypress can grow very slowly, giving it a stunted look and earning it the name "dwarf cypress" or "hat rack cypress." This tree grows in quiet, still, or lazy, slow-moving water. The lower part of both tree trunks are fluted, probably because the roots are so near the surface of the soil.

This beautiful little swamp is on Highway 231, north of Montgomery, Alabama, and just about 15 miles from my home.

Cypress trees can fool you into thinking they are much older than they really are. Their growth rings are not true indications of the years; instead, they indicate the rise and fall of the water level, which sometimes produces two or three rings in a year. Cat Island Swamp in north central Louisiana is the home of the National Champion Cypress, which holds two titles: the largest of the bald cypress trees and the largest tree east of California's Sierra Nevada range. It is 53 feet in circumference and 90 feet tall. Its age is estimated at 700 to more than 1000 years old.

Cypress is used in many different ways—for building houses, ships, and even coffins. In 1 Kings in the Bible, we are told that King Solomon built his palace from cedar and cypress.

Most people find that the roots of cypress trees are the most interesting aspect of the trees. Because the roots are so shallow, they intertwine with the trees around them, making it very unlikely that hurricane winds will blow them over. The curious thing

about the roots is the exquisite upward growths, called knees, that reach above the water level. No two are alike, and no one knows just what their purpose is. Some think they snorkel air to the root. Others think they anchor and balance the tree. Some think they store starches. Still others think they are pneumatophores, a way for the tree to draw in oxygen. My own personal opinion is that God made them just for our pleasure. Whatever their purpose, there is no evidence that removing the knees is harmful to the trees. The trees continue to grow and thrive and produce more knees.

Cypress knees can grow from a few inches in height to 12 feet, depending on the depth of the water level. The largest one I've carved was 5 feet 4 inches tall. In general, the knees are much lighter in color and the wood is softer (to the point of sometimes being punky) than that of the tree trunk.

Getting the bark off the knees can be a real problem, so I leave that to the experts. Some people boil the knees, and then strip the bark off while the wood is still hot. Others steam the knees before stripping them. Either way, once the bark is stripped away, you can see the lovely shapes that have been hidden all these years.

As the knees dry, they form what I call a "skin." This skin is usually about as thick as your fingernail and just about that hard. The wood inside is a soft, easily worked wood, but for some people, getting through that skin can be exasperating. It is difficult to carve cross-grain, and some tearing and crushing are likely to occur. Power tools are a good solution for this situation.

Some people like the look of a cypress knee but don't like carving actual cypress knees. For these folks, basswood blanks shaped like cypress knees provide the perfect medium.

Carving Basics

My style of carving is a little different, so I recommend that you read this entire book before you start carving in order to understand my style a little better. I don't really carve realistically, although there is a lot of realism in what I do. I combine realistic, caricature, and primitive aspects of a subject to create my style.

Measurements and style

Generally speaking, most of the faces I carve are longer than what would be correct realistically. Many of the Old World Father Christmas figures that you see have long, thin, gaunt faces, and that just appeals to me. As long as people like what I do, I won't worry about exact measurements. Most people don't have perfect faces anyway.

In this chapter, you'll find an illustration of some of the measurements that I use in

my carvings (see **Figure 2.1**). Some are anatomically correct and some may not be, but my carvings are close enough to being realistic that people puzzle over just exactly how to classify them.

All of the pieces in this book were done using the same steps, but, as you see, they all look different. That's the fun of carving. Here are some tips to help you get started:

- Learn to block out the shapes before you start to carve. If the overall shape is pleasing, you know you can go ahead and finish the piece.
- Learn to trust your eyes. If it doesn't look right to you, it probably isn't, but don't throw it away. Learn to fix it. That's how you grow.
- Don't work in one area too long. Work all over the piece.
- Cypress knees are fun to work with but are very different than most wood. They are softwood, but that doesn't necessarily

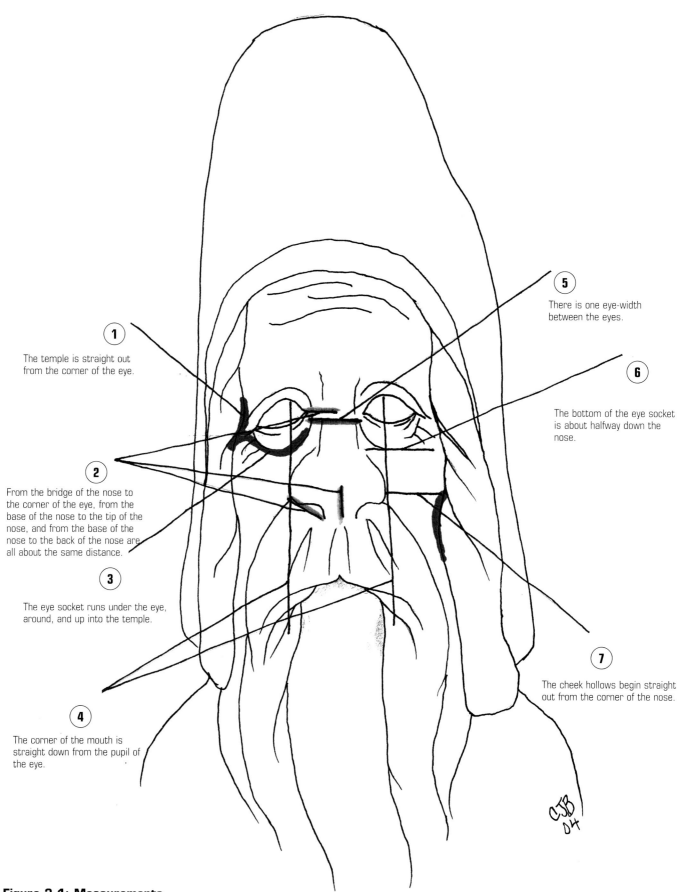

1 The temple is straight out from the corner of the eye.

2 From the bridge of the nose to the corner of the eye, from the base of the nose to the tip of the nose, and from the base of the nose to the back of the nose are all about the same distance.

3 The eye socket runs under the eye, around, and up into the temple.

4 The corner of the mouth is straight down from the pupil of the eye.

5 There is one eye-width between the eyes.

6 The bottom of the eye socket is about halfway down the nose.

7 The cheek hollows begin straight out from the corner of the nose.

Figure 2.1: Measurements
This illustration shows the general measurements I use to create a face. These measurements are based on real faces, but they are not exact.

mean "easy." It is very difficult to carve cross-grain. The wood will crush and tear. A power chisel is most helpful.

- Cypress knees are truly the most forgiving wood around. You can sand out little imperfections amazingly fast.
- Keep your tools sharp. Always slice, carving from the heel of your knife to the tip.

Tools

I guess I'm basically what you would call a whittler. I use my knife for everything I can make it do, and that's a lot. I use a couple of large-blade knives (Helvies), a push knife made by the late Preacher Bledsole years ago, and a wonderful little detail knife made by George Vaughn (see **Photo 2.1**). I probably have at least 30 knives and use them all for one thing or another. I still don't have the perfect knife though. Do you? If you find it, let me know!

I do think you should use the tools that are comfortable for you. Throughout this book, I'll show you what I do and how I go about it. If you can achieve the same result with another tool, that's fine.

In addition to good knives, I have found two other hand tools that are of great use when carving cypress knees: a little shallow U-gouge with "Harmon" written on the back and a small skew tool with "Nauger Nob" written on the back. A pair of dividers is also very handy. Of course, you must always have a good strop, leather thumb guards, a carving glove, goggles, and a nailbrush, to brush away chips and dust.

Power tools aren't required to carve cypress knees, but they are a big help. I use a power chisel fitted with a Flexcut blade and a rotary tool with an array of bits, including a circular saw bit and pear- and flame-shaped bits, among others. A magnetized dish keeps all of the bits in one place. I also

Photo 2.1 Good quality, very sharp hand tools are necessary for carving cypress knees. Power tools, such as a rotary tool and a power chisel are handy, but not required.

use a woodburner. I don't suppose I'll ever have enough tools. I always want to try the new ones, don't you? For information on where to find some of the tools listed here, try your local woodworking supply store or refer to the Resources section on page 89.

Painting tips

My professional background before coming to the world of woodcarving was as a photographic artist. What that means is that I retouched the negative and then painted the photograph in both light oils and heavy oils when we only had black and white photography. Then, when color photography hit the scene, I retouched both the negative and the print. Because of this background, I paint my carvings a little differently than most people.

Just a word about paints and colors: I use all the different brand names. The color may vary a little bit in different brands, but that doesn't really make a big difference to me. The biggest favor you can do yourself is to buy a color wheel and get really familiar with it.

First of all, I paint keeping in mind what good lighting will do for the piece that I'm working on and then work toward achieving

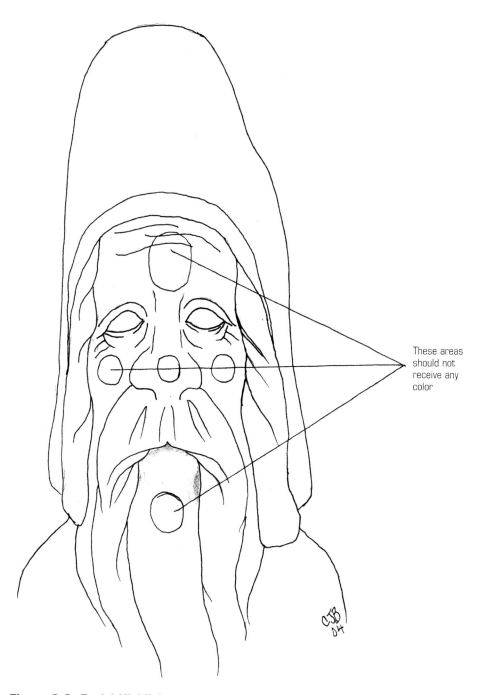

These areas should not receive any color

Figure 2.2: Facial Highlights
The five areas circled here—the forehead, both cheeks, the tip of the nose, and the chin—are highlight areas and should receive no color.

that look. In almost any light, you will have five main highlight areas on the face. These are found in the middle of the forehead, at the end of the nose, in the middle of the chin, and at the highest part of both cheeks (see **Figure 2.2**). Make yourself consciously aware of these areas at all times when you are painting the face. You don't want to put any color in these areas.

I paint in very thin washes, going back over any given area as many times as I need to get the depth of color that I want. It's much better to start too light, because you can always add more, but it's difficult to take off. I paint in transparent washes because I want the wood grain to show through the color.

Painting Blue Eyes

I start by using acrylic paint for the eyes.

1. Thin white acrylic paint until it is watery.

2. Paint the entire eyeball, being careful not to get any paint on the eyelids. (If your paint is too thick, the color will be too white. Most people don't have really white eyeballs.)

3. Using a hair dryer, dry well.

4. Then, using Figure 2.3 as a guide, paint the iris a nice dark blue. Remember that part of the iris is hidden under the top eyelid, and the bottom of the iris meets the bottom eyelid. Don't make a little round ball with white showing all the way around it or the piece will have a frightened look.

5. Using a hair dryer, dry well.

6. Using light blue paint (see Figure 2.4), brush some color on the left side and bottom of both eyes. Stay inside the dark blue.

7. Using a hair dryer, dry well.

8. Paint the pupil black, as shown in Figure 2.5. Paint the black right over the light blue, leaving just a thin crescent of light blue showing. I make large pupils because it gives the finished piece a kind, sweet look. If you make the pupils too small, the finished piece will look mean.

9. Using a hair dryer, dry well.

10. This last step is what really wakes him up. Using Figure 2.6 as a guide, put just a small white dot of paint in the one o'clock or two o'clock position of both eyes. It must be in the same spot in both eyes. If you get this step right, the eyes will seem to follow you from one side of the room to the other.

Different Eye Color

Use the chart below and follow the steps in Figures 2.3, 2.4, 2.5, and 2.6 to create eyes of different colors.

	Blue	**Brown**	**Green**
Figure 2.3	Blue (iris)	Brown (iris)	Green (iris)
Figure 2.4	Light blue (reflected light)	Orange, yellow, or copper (reflected light)	Yellow or gold (reflected light)
Figure 2.5	Black (pupil)	Black (pupil)	Black (pupil)
Figure 2.6	White (highlight)	White (highlight)	White (highlight)

That being said, there are always some areas that need to be opaque. The eyes are one of those areas. I always start by using acrylic paint for these places (see **Figures 2.3, 2.4, 2.5,** and **2.6** and the sidebar, **"Painting Blue Eyes"**). While you have the acrylic paint out, go ahead and paint any trim or other embellishment that you have. Then, put your acrylic paints away.

Now the real fun begins. We're going to switch to oil paint. Most flesh-color paint that you buy really doesn't look like flesh, so I don't use it. It's amazing how many woods almost have a flesh color to them when finished, especially cypress knees. I let the wood, by itself, be my base flesh color and then just add blush and shading where it's needed (see **Figure 2.7** and the sidebar, **"Creating Flesh Tones"**).

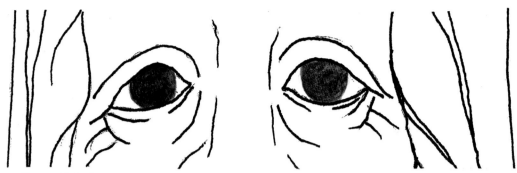

Figure 2.3: Iris
The iris is painted as a solid circle of color. Note that the top of the iris seems to disappear under the upper eyelid, and the bottom of the iris meets the bottom eyelid.

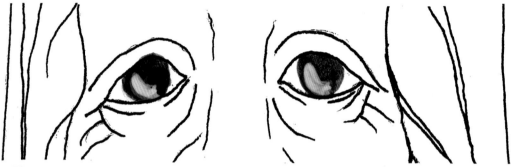

Figure 2.4: Reflected Light
A semicircle of reflected light—generally a lighter or complementary color to the iris—occupies the bottom and left sides of the iris.

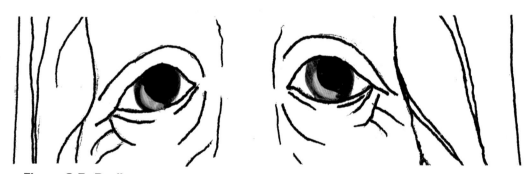

Figure 2.5: Pupil
A circle of black that just covers the inside edge of the reflected light serves as the pupil.

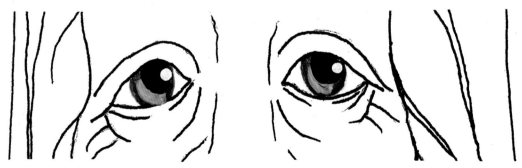

Figure 2.6: Highlight
A dot of white in the one or two o'clock position, partly on the black and partly on the blue, highlights each eye and gives the eye life.

When you have finished painting the whole piece and have sprayed it with Deft Semi-Gloss, you will be amazed at what a beautiful flesh color you have created.

Figure 2.8 shows the final face with the hair roughed in. Spraying will change the color of the wood.

Figure 2.7: Flesh Tones
The base flesh tone is provided by the hue of the cypress knee itself. A mix of thinned-down vermilion and burnt sienna gives the face additional color.

Creating Flesh Tones

I've found that leaving the wood bare, especially on cypress knees, provides a great flesh-colored base. The directions below and Figure 2.7 will help you to bring out the highlights, to blush and shade, and to create a realistic look.

1 In a jar lid, mix a little vermilion with just a smidge of burnt sienna. If you can't find vermilion, use cadmium red.

2 Using mineral spirits, thin this mixture until it's liquid—just a thin wash.

3 Wet the figure's cheeks with mineral spirits, keeping the spirits out of the highlight areas of his cheeks (see Figure 2.2). The mineral spirits will let the paint feather and blend easier in a large area.

4 Now dip a #3 or a #4 round brush into your paint mixture. Test it on a white paper towel to be sure you don't have too much paint on your brush.

5 Very lightly, brush it on the cheeks in a U shape around the highlight areas. Make sure to keep it out of the highlight areas.

6 Quickly blend the edges of the color with the ball of your finger, remembering to stay out of the highlight. Use Figure 2.7 as your guide.

7 As the paint dries, it will become lighter and you may find that you need to add more color, but wait until it's dry to check.

8 Using a smaller round brush, put color in all of the areas shown in Figure 2.7: in the fold of the eyelids, under the eyebrows, in the corner of the eyes, and along the edges of the bottom eyelids. Brush just a little in all the wrinkles and between the eyebrows. Shade just a little under the edge of the hood. Brush a little, ever so lightly, along the sides of the nose and in the crease of the flare of the nose. Paint just a tiny bit across and above the ball of the nose, *not* on the tip of the nose. Put some under the nose and inside the nostrils. Stay out of the highlight area on the tip of the nose. Brush a little on his lip and blend it quickly with your finger. You don't want to see a lip line on a man.

Figure 2.8: Creating Hair
Use this illustration as a guide when you get ready to burn the eyebrows, hair, moustache, and beard. This is how I begin to get the overall flow before filling it all in. Except for the eyebrows, all hair grows down first; then it can wave and curl.

Design and Composition

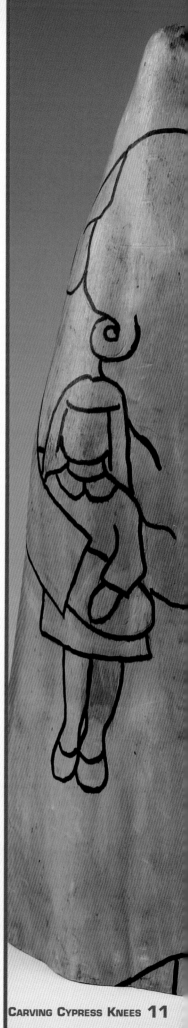

When you first start thinking about carving a cypress knee, all kinds of things will go through your mind. Because there are all kinds of lumps and bumps, it's easy to see an eye or a nose or maybe even a chin—a lot of other things, too. If all you are going to do is paint it, that's great. I have seen some very good-looking painted cypress knees. However, this book is about carving. Because of that, you have to look at the knees in a different way.

The grain on a cypress knee goes in all different directions, especially where there are bumps and ripples. So, you'll want to start the design and composition process by looking for a smooth, clear place to put the face. The smoother it is, the straighter the grain will be, and the less chance you have of losing a nose because the grain changed.

For example, if you are planning to carve a figure with shoulders, such as a Father Christmas, you should select a knee that has an A shape to it. You know the shoulders have to be wider than the head, so if you choose an A-shaped knee, you will already have the shoulders there.

Once you know where the top of the head is (not the top of the hat or the top of the hood, but the top of the head), measure from the top of the head to the bottom of the cypress knee. Mark the halfway spot. That is where the crotch is. The figure's fingertips should not be any lower than mid-thigh. Make sure both arms are the same length and width. The rest of the anatomy should take care of itself because it's all hidden under Father Christmas's coat.

I try to keep the rippled part in the back, especially when I'm carving Father Christmas, because it can be used for a toy bag or a backpack. There are a lot of different things that you can do with that part. Just use your imagination. Find ways

Photo 3.1
There are many things for your eyes to explore on this piece. As you look at his face, you will naturally follow the beard all the way down, and then the curl at the bottom will bring your eyes right back up to the face.

Photo 3.2
As in the photo above, the curl at the bottom of the beard will lead you right back to the face. Also, as you inspect the elf, the angle of Santa's arm will lead you right back to Santa's face.

to add a doll, a teddy bear, an open toy bag, a dollhouse, a drum, a ball, a puppy or a kitten, skates, and candy canes.

Other bumps and ripples can turn into more design features. You can put a wreath or a walking stick or anything else you fancy in Father Christmas's hand. Just remember that whatever you design has to be appropriate timewise. A ball, a bell, or a toy horse will work; a basketball, a football, an airplane, or a car won't.

Let his coat be open to show his gown, or close it to show some large gold buttons. You can make fur trim or gold braid trim…so many different things. Look for old Christmas cards; they will give you a lot of inspiration.

The face of your carving should always be the main source of interest. You want people to look at everything else on your carving, but their eyes need to always go back to the face. For instance, you can use the curls in the beard to bring the eye back up to the face. A good example of this is seen in **Photo 3.1**. Even though the beard leads you away from the face, the curl at the bottom brings your eye right back up to the face. Another example is seen in **Photo 3.2.** You can't help looking at the elf, but the angle of Santa's arm brings you right back up to the face.

You also want to be sure to keep the piece well balanced, but that does not mean that the figure has to be the same on both sides. As you are drawing your design on the cypress knee, make yourself think about how

all these lines should be laid out in order to keep the face the main focus of interest. Draw the design on with pencil first because you may need to rethink it and make changes a few times before you are pleased with it. Notice that I don't draw on the face—you need to see it in your head as you carve it. Sometimes there are little lumps and bumps that you just can't use. When that happens, go ahead and carve them off so they won't be in your way.

Let's look at a couple more examples. When you are looking for a knee to carve into an elf's head, you again need an A-shaped cypress knee so that you can make the elf's ears stand out. I like to give the elf really large ears so that everyone knows immediately that this piece is an elf. When you are selecting a cypress knee for a "knee spirit," you can use almost any shape you want. One that really has a lot of lumps, bumps, and ripples on one side and is nice and smooth on the other side is perfect. You want to leave the bumpy side alone and carve the face on the plain side. This will make it really interesting.

Because every knee is different, I can't provide patterns. Instead, on the following pages, I'm going to give you pictures of some knees on which I've already drawn a pattern. Study these drawings carefully (see **Pattern Practice 1** to **Pattern Practice 8**). Then, study the pictures of the knees on the inside covers of this book. Once you've studied both sets of pictures, you can make copies of the blank knees and design your own patterns. You could also try tracing the outline of the knees onto tracing paper, and then drawing the patterns.

Pattern Practice 1

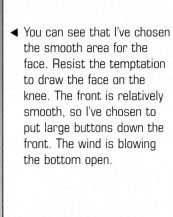

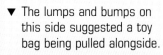

◄ You can see that I've chosen the smooth area for the face. Resist the temptation to draw the face on the knee. The front is relatively smooth, so I've chosen to put large buttons down the front. The wind is blowing the bottom open.

► You can see the toy bag behind him as well.

▼ The lumps and bumps on this side suggested a toy bag being pulled alongside.

▼ Here you can see that the angle of the teddy bear will lead the eyes back to Santa's face.

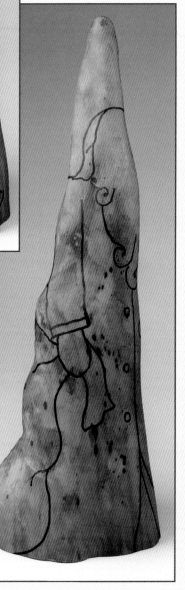

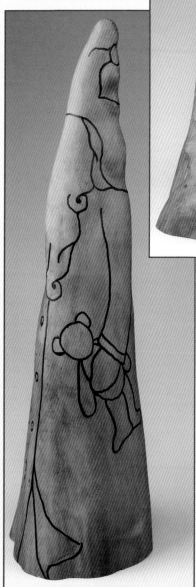

Pattern Practice 2

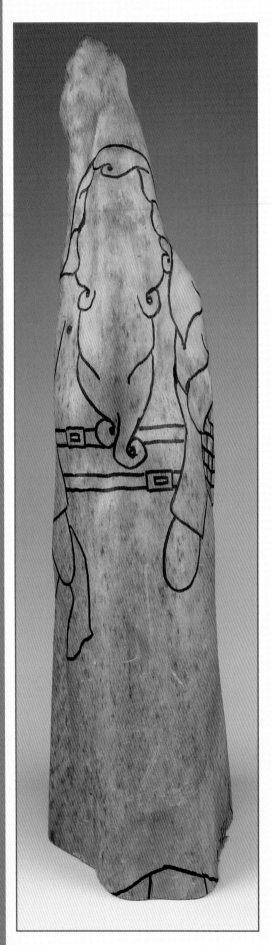

◄ A clear spot for the face was chosen with lots of room for waves and curls in his hair. A foot is peeking out from under his coat.

▼ You can see from this side that I ended his beard where I did because of the extra material on the side. Since this side was larger than the other, a tree sitting in a basket that was strapped around his waist seemed to be a good choice.

▼ From this side you can see that he is dragging his toy bag behind.

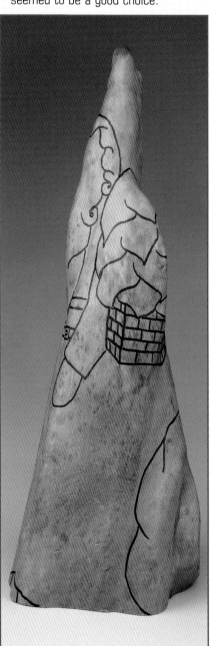

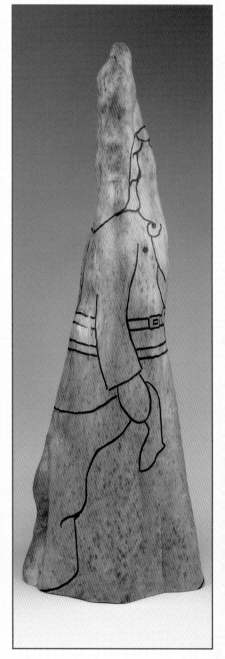

Pattern Practice 3

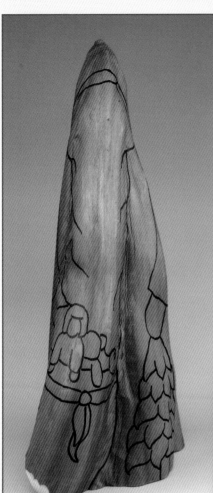

◀ Again a clear spot for the face was chosen. The shape suggests a very long beard going all the way down behind his toy bag, which is open to show some toys.

▼ There is enough wood on this side to put a small tree in his hand.

▼ The flaw at the bottom will become part of the bag.

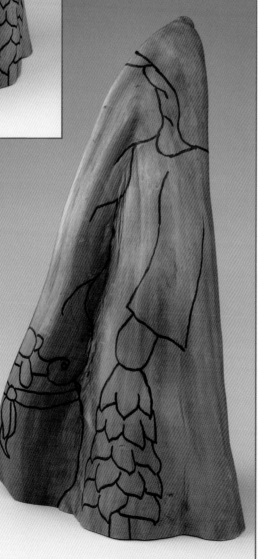

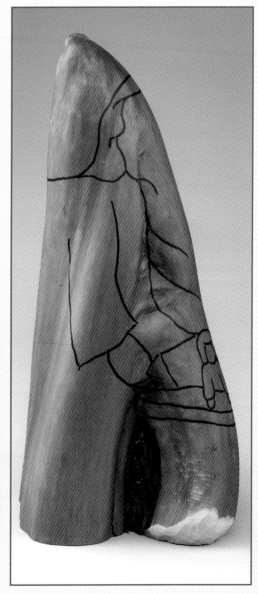

Pattern Practice 4

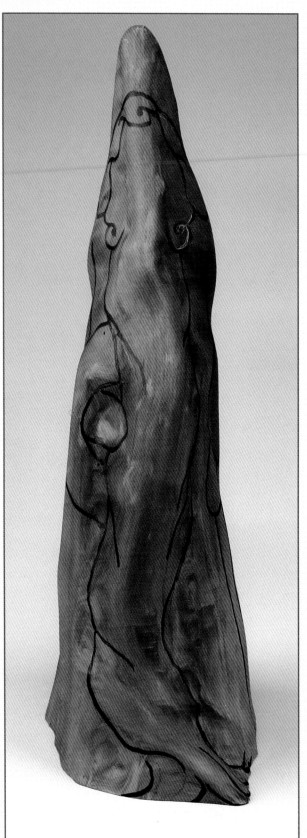

◀ This one really has a long flowing beard.

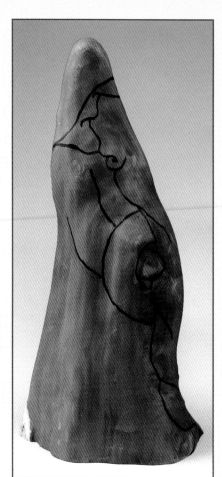

▶ From this side you can see how far out in front the beard is and that it would be too thick, so I included a wreath under the beard.

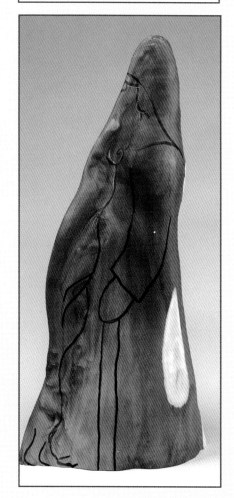

▶ On this side, he is leaning on a walking stick. You can see where I carved off an unneeded little lump.

Pattern Practice 5

▶ This knee really has a lot of lumps and bumps to use and would offer a little more challenge than some of the others. There is a good clear spot for the face, but the teddy bear out in front must be carved first. The beard runs down behind the teddy.

▲ You can see how far in front the lump for the teddy bear is. You could also put a wreath or walking stick in his hand.

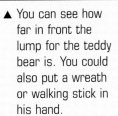

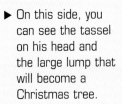

▶ On this side, you can see the tassel on his head and the large lump that will become a Christmas tree.

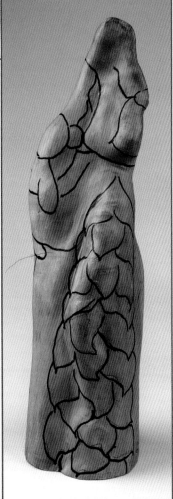

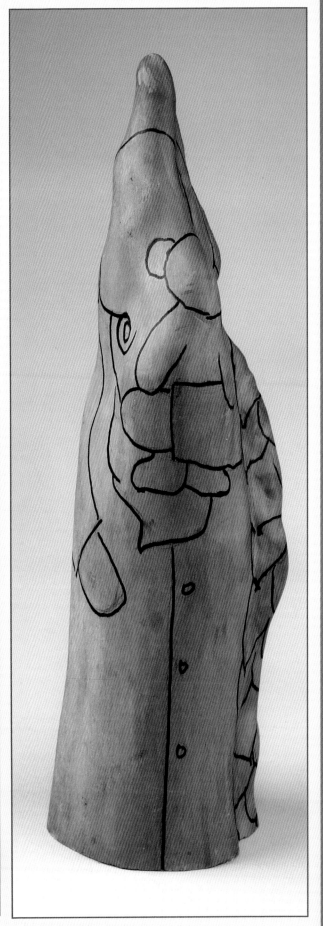

Pattern Practice 6

▼ It's easy to see that the toy bag is right out in front, and the beard is lying right on top of the bag. You can see that he is holding the top of the toy bag in his left hand.

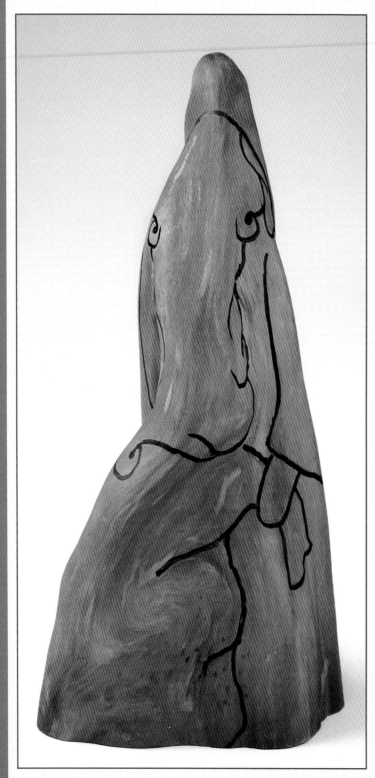

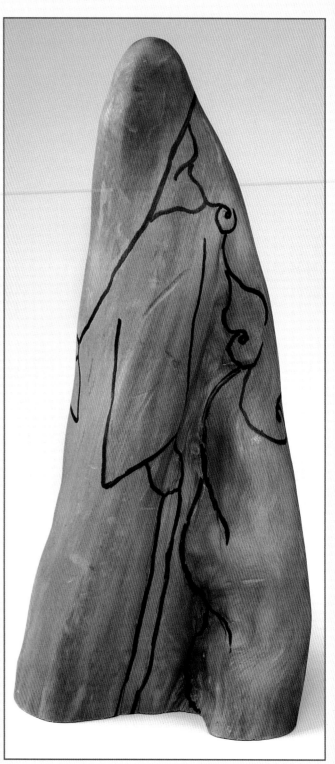

▲ He's using a walking stick in his right hand to help him along the way.

Pattern Practice 7

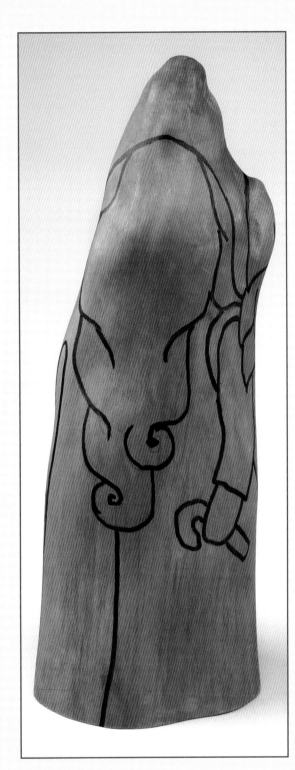

◄ This one will have a wide, fat face, and it looks like he might have a handlebar moustache hiding in there.

▼ On this side, you see a teddy bear hanging from the top of the bag and a walking stick in his hand.

▼ You can see that the bag on this one is worn as a backpack with a tree poking out the top of the bag. He carries a candy cane in his hand.

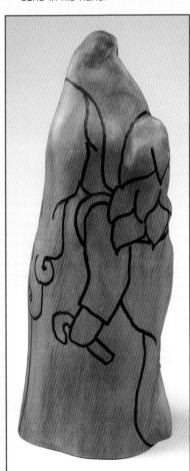

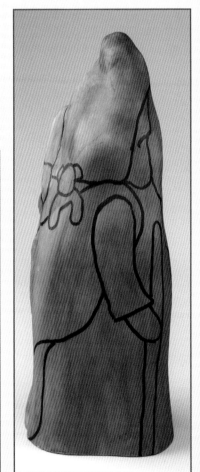

Pattern Practice 8

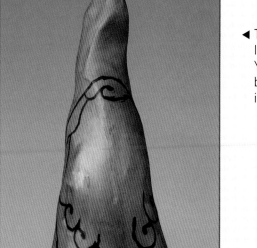

◄ This one is quite a round fellow—just look what a round face is indicated. You can tell exactly where the curly beard will end. He seems to be walking with his foot out in front.

▼ You can see from the side exactly where the wreath should go.

▼ Of course it takes both hands to carry this large wreath.

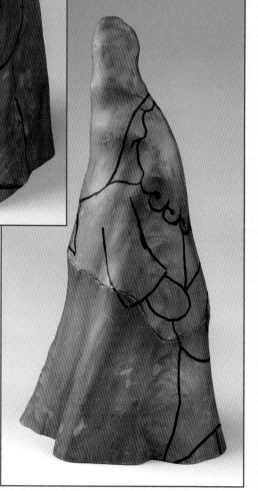

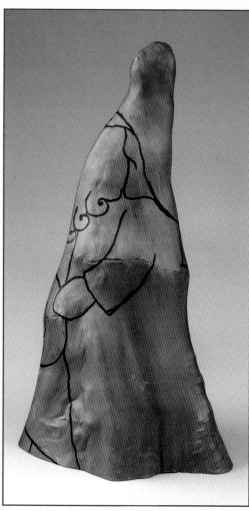

Gallery

In this section, I wanted to include both my own carvings and some pieces of my students to give you the encouragement to jump in and try carving cypress knees. You'll notice that I have not included names for the pieces shown here. I don't usually give my carvings specific names because I get too attached to them, and then I have a hard time letting them go. I can't tell you which one is my favorite because each time I complete a new knee, it becomes my favorite. You can see from this picture that they come in all shapes and sizes. All of them were carved using the same steps given in this book (with the exception of the ones that are laughing or showing teeth) yet you'll notice how different they look. Someone once told me, "They all look different, but they look like brothers." Then, he laughed and said, "And you look like their mother." As you look at these photographs, pay attention to the beauty of the wood grain. Isn't it lovely? Look at the differences in the way the hair and beards are handled, and notice the trim, just small splashes of gold or copper and a few bright berries. There is not too much of any one thing, just bright splashes. I hope that you enjoy them all, and let me know which ones are your favorites.

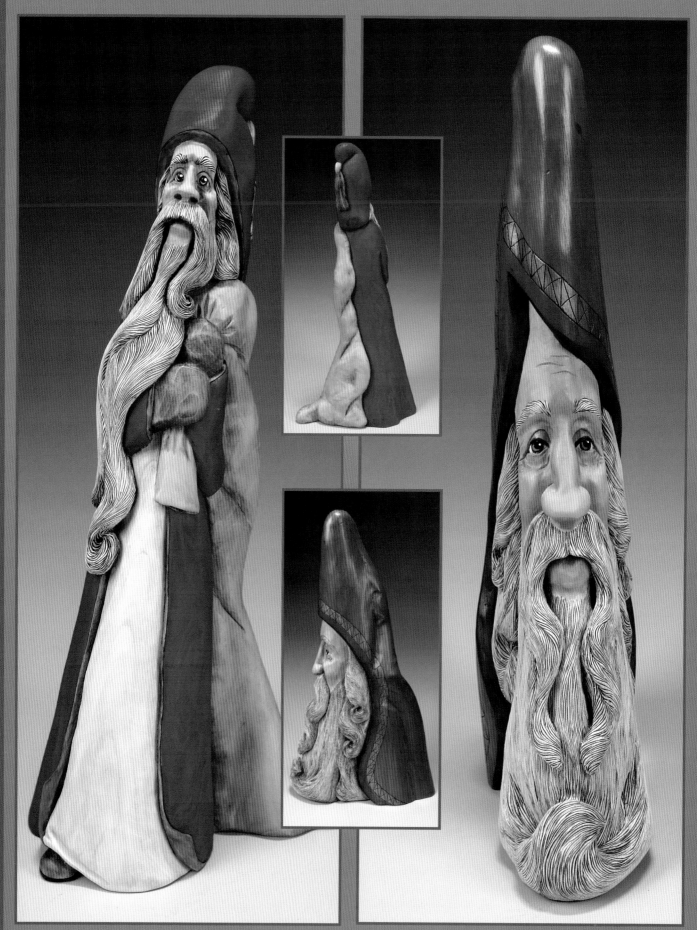

In the collection of Dr. and Mrs. Chris Magee.

In the collection of Debrah A. Stenner.

In the collection of Ted and Linda Frick.

In the collection of Wendi Ericksen.

Collection unknown.

In the collection of Lee and Sandra Christensen.

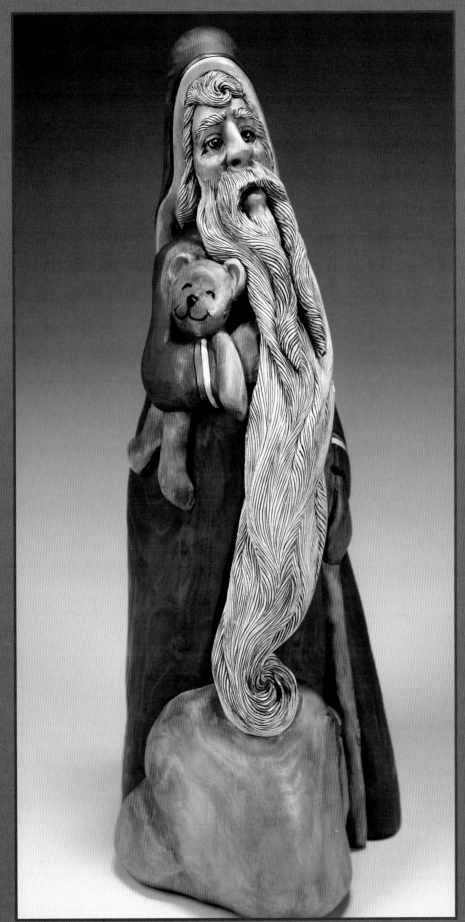

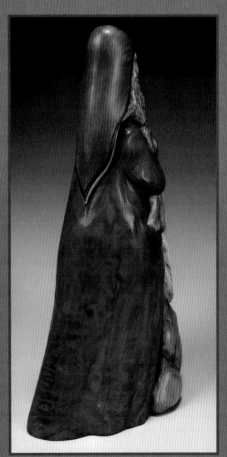

In the collection of Dr. Richard C. McConnell.

In the collection of Timothy & Marcia Wise.

In the collection of Trica Taylor.

In the collection of Dr. and Mrs. Chris Magee.

In the collection of Laura Baxter.

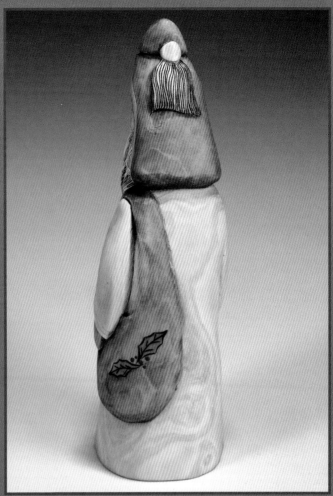

In the collection of Betty Snyder.

In the collection of Linda O'Banion.

In the collection of Cathy Price.

In the collection of Larry Lucree.

In the collection of Allen & Lynda Carmichael.

In the collection of Bob and Linda Harris.

In the collection of Bob and Linda Harris.

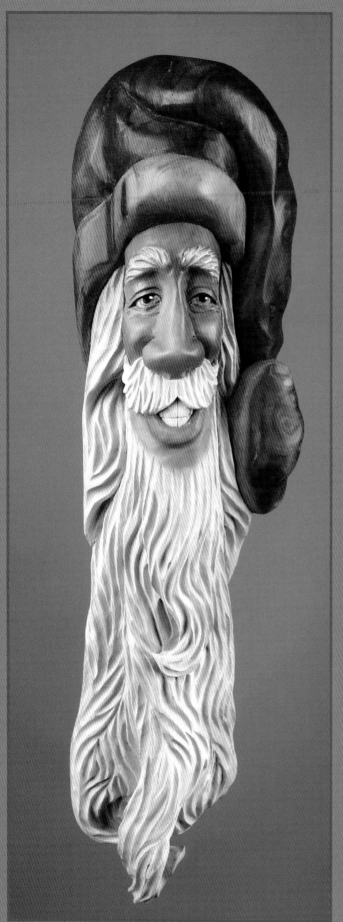

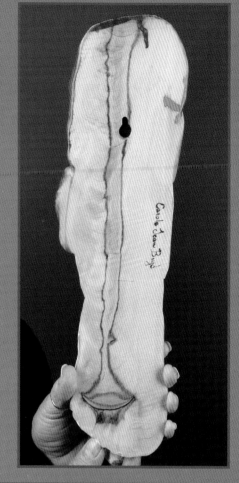

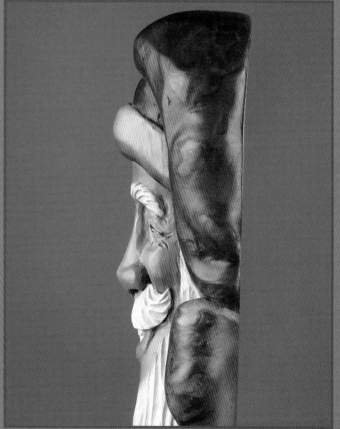

In the collection of Allen & Lynda Carmichael.

In the collection of Teresa Kendrick (5 feet, 4 inches tall).

In the collection of Dr. and Mrs. Chris Magee.

Carved by Willie Stewart (student).

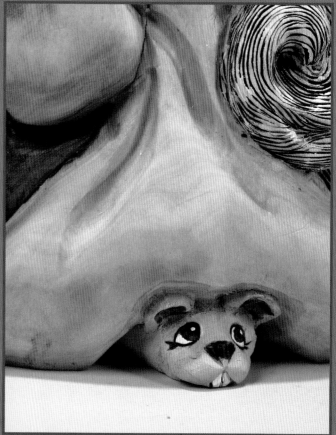

Carved by Floyd Rhadigan (student).

Carved by students Willie Stewart (left), Greg Price (middle), and Floyd Rhadigan (right).

Carving a Knee Spirit

A knee spirit is pure fun and fantasy. Use your imagination and let your creativity run wild! You want him to look lifelike, but you also want him to appear to live inside the confines of the knee. I've seen a lot of different styles, some very stern and mean-looking, but I prefer to give him a kind, gentle personality.

You can use these same steps to make a face using any kind of wood. If you are a little hesitant to try a cypress knee, try it first on the kind of wood that you enjoy carving. Just have fun carving faces. Each one will be different and have his own personality.

Materials List

Wood
Cypress knee or wood of choice

Supplies
Pencil and permanent marker
Rotary tool with circular saw bit, a large pear-shaped diamond or ruby bit, and a flame- or tear-shaped bit
Power chisel
Knife of choice
U-gouge
Cloth-backed sandpaper, 220–400 grit
Eye punch
Dividers
Paintbrushes: round, sizes #1, #3, and #5 flat, sizes #2, #4, and #6
Hair dryer
Mineral spirits
Deft semi-gloss clear spray

Acrylic Paints
White
Brown
Metallic copper
Black

Oil Paints
Vermilion
Burnt sienna

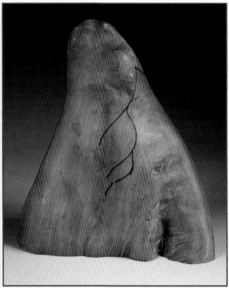

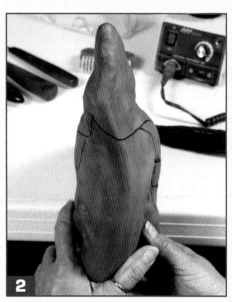

1 This is the first knee that we will be working on, as seen from the front and side. We will be carving what I call a Knee Spirit. Keep in mind that we want this grizzled old man to appear to live inside the knee.

2 Looking at the knee from the top front, you want to be sure that you have drawn the pattern evenly on both sides.

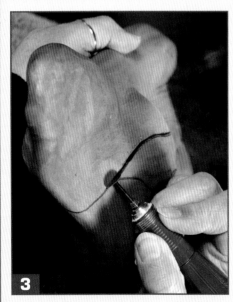

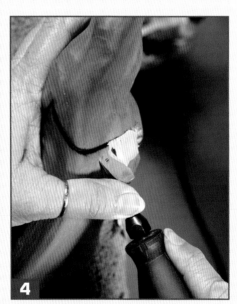

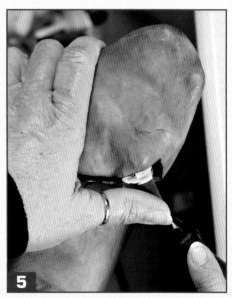

3 This little bit fitted in my rotary tool is just a little circular saw. It makes a good, deep stop cut, though it will sometimes burn as it cuts.

4 The deep cut made by the circular saw bit also makes it easy to carve back to the stop cut with a power chisel—without getting a lot of fuzzies.

5 Be sure to make deep cuts in the point where the part in the Spirit's hair will be. I use a power chisel for a lot of the work here.

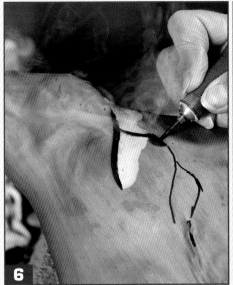

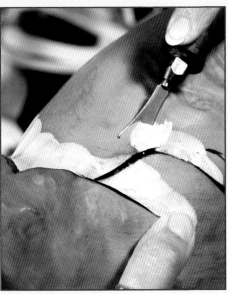

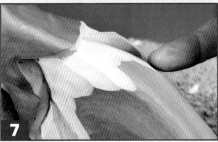

6

After you've carved the opening, stop cut the first layer of hair with the circular saw bit. Don't make the stop cuts for all of the layers at the same time. Carve one layer at a time and make each layer deeper than you think you should.

7

As you look at the piece from the front, you should be able to see all the layers of hair. Notice how deep each layer of hair is carved. Now trim off any burn marks that were left by the circular saw bit.

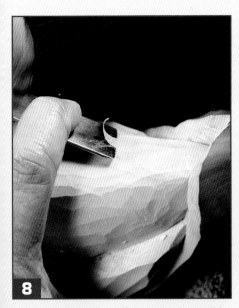

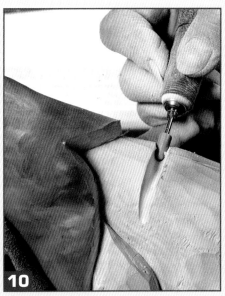

8

Carve all of the skin off the area that will be the face. Be sure to leave the skin on everything except where the face, hair, and beard will be.

9

Draw the centerline, following the curve of the knee. Now draw an arched line across the face to indicate the brow line. This line should not go all the way to the hairline.

10

Using the rotary tool and a large pear-shaped diamond or ruby bit, follow the arch line for the brow. You can see how deep the bit is into the wood.

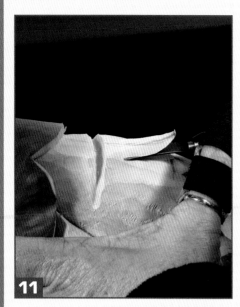

11

Using the power chisel and following the centerline, carve straight up from about where the end of the nose will be to the brow line, making the cut gradually deeper as you approach the brow line.

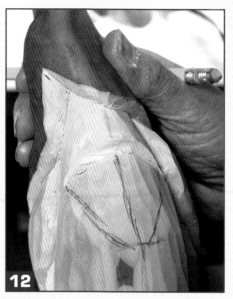

12

Redraw the centerline. Now draw a line where you want the end of the nose to be. The placement of this line will vary according to the size and shape of the knee that you are carving. I like to make large, impressive noses. Now draw a line from the end of the nose to the corner of the brow line. It is better to make the nose too large because it will get smaller as you carve it.

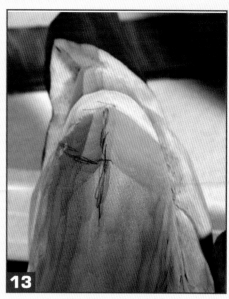

13

Do not cut off the centerline again. Using the power chisel, carve off the pie-shaped wedge on each side of the centerline. That should give you the shape you see here. This is the beginning of the ridge of the nose.

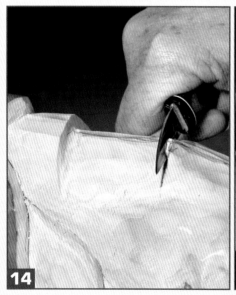

14

With a knife, make a stop cut at the bottom of the nose. This cut should angle toward the mouth. Be careful not to cut in or back, or you'll have a hooked nose. Remove the wood under the nose, creating a shape similar to that under the brow (see Step 13). Remember that this area is not flat; instead, it curves back around the face.

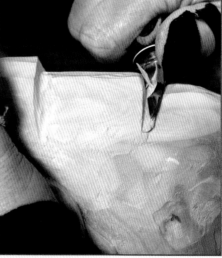

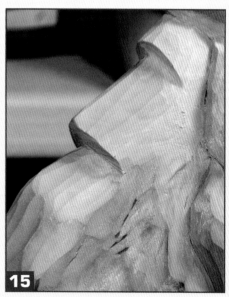

15

You can see that you need to carve more depth here than you did under the brow.

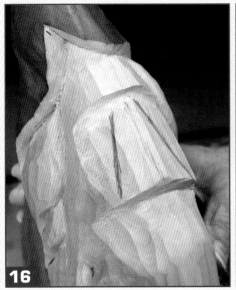
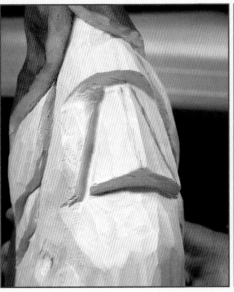
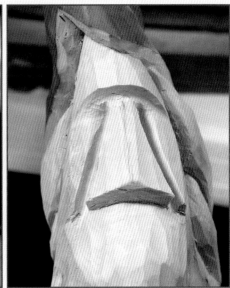

Draw a line from the corner of the bottom of the nose at an angle up to the brow. Using the large pear-shaped bit, carve a groove at an angle down from the brow to the corner of the nose, making this a deep cut.

You can see in this photo how the nose wraps around the face. It's not just sitting on the end of the face. You can also see how deep the cut is coming down the side of the nose.

Draw a line about halfway down the nose, out to the side of the face. This is the bottom of the eye socket. As you carve away the excess wood on both sides of the nose, try not to go above the pencil line.

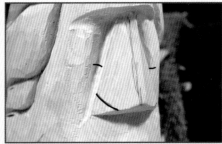
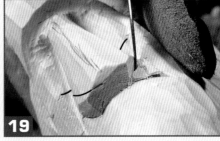

Draw a line from the base of the nose at an angle to the side of the nose. Make a stop cut with a knife and take this little corner off. Be sure to carve off all the little cuts left from the corner.

20

Trim the corner edge of the nose all the way up to the brow.

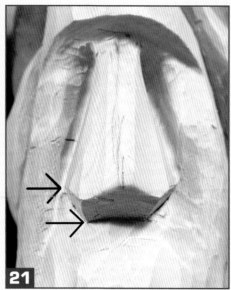

21

This is the shape you should have now. As much of the nose should be sitting back on the face as is sitting out in front of the face. The arrows mark the high corner and the low corner of the nose.

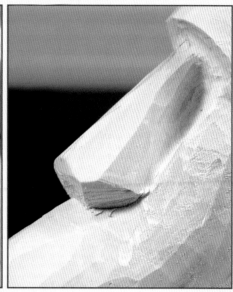

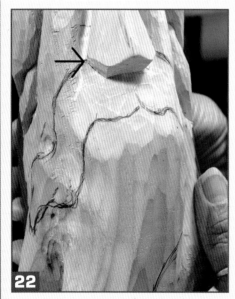

22

You are ready now to draw on the Knee Spirit's moustache. Keep in mind that the corners of the mouth are in a straight line down from the pupils of the eyes (see Chapter Two, Figure 2.1). It's fun to make a great, long, flowing moustache—just remember to leave room for the mouth. The moustache should start at the high corner of the nose.

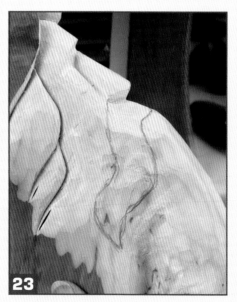

23

Looking at the profile, you can see that a lot of wood needs to be removed under the moustache. The moustache will always overhang the bottom lip.

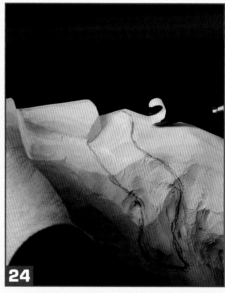

24

Before you make the stop cut around the moustache, go ahead and remove some of this wood. We'll get the rest later.

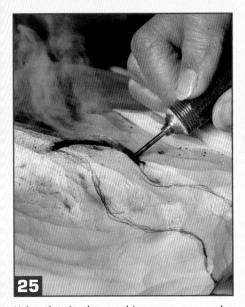

25 Using the circular saw bit, stop cut around the bottom of the moustache.

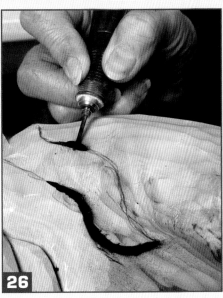

26 Stay away from the areas above and below the lips when using the saw. The saw bit is too aggressive to use near the face or the lips.

27 Using the knife, stop cut under the moustache.

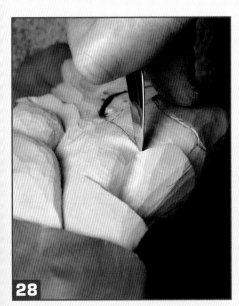

28 Stop cut around the top of the moustache as well. Make this a good, deep cut.

29 Quite a lot of wood needs to be removed as you carve up the inside of the moustache to the corner of the mouth. I use a power chisel in this area.

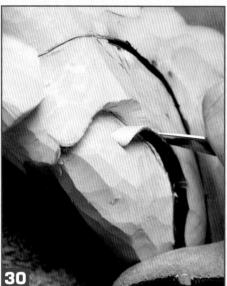

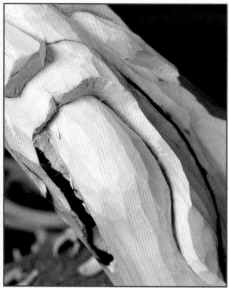

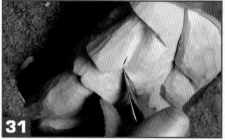

30

Switching back to a knife, continue to remove wood so that the lip appears to be behind the moustache. This area is not flat, so be sure to round it back under the moustache. Trim off any burn marks caused by the saw. Notice how thick the moustache is. You'll see why you need this thickness later.

31

Make a deep stop cut with the knife from the high corner of the nose about one-third of the way up the nose. From that same corner, make sure the stop cut across the top of the moustache is good and deep.

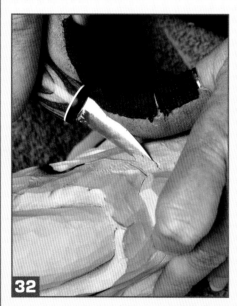

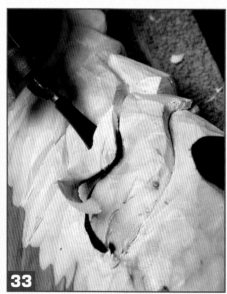

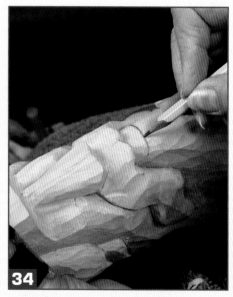

32

Start to carve down to the moustache about one-fourth of the way up the nose. This should be a fairly deep cut, and, if you've made a good stop cut, the excess wood should easily come loose.

33

With the power chisel, continue carving down the entire moustache. Be sure to carve deeply all the way around the moustache so it will lie nicely on top of the beard.

34

Draw in the Knee Spirit's lip. Make it a nice plump one; skinny lips will make the finished piece look mean. Do not make a stop cut here with your knife.

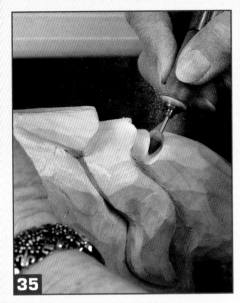

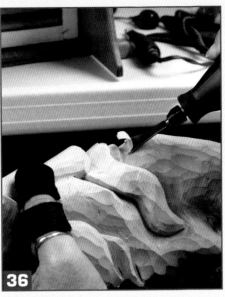

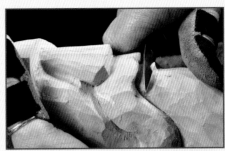

35 Using the large pear-shaped bit, carve a deep groove on the lip line. In this photograph, you can see just how deep the bit is in the wood. If you don't use power tools, use a deep U-gouge—don't make a stop cut with the knife.

36 Remove the excess wood under the lip with the power chisel. Remember this area is not flat. Round it back under the moustache to indicate a chin.

Use a knife to round and smooth the lip, being sure not to make any definite lines. A man's lip should not be well defined.

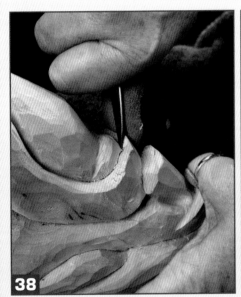

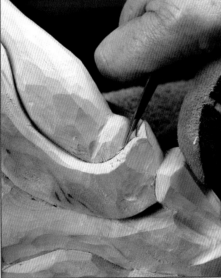

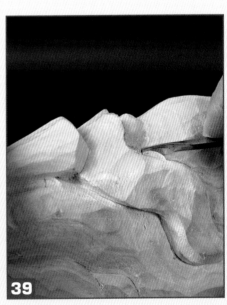

38 Make a deep stop cut with the knife between the lip and the moustache. Now carve out just a little sliver of wood. This indicates a separation between the top and bottom lip.

39 Using a U-gouge, make a cut just under the lip and before the beard that cuts back toward the moustache. This finishes the lip.

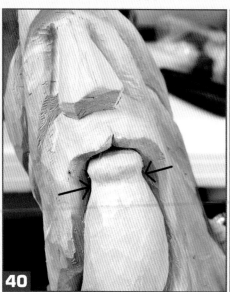

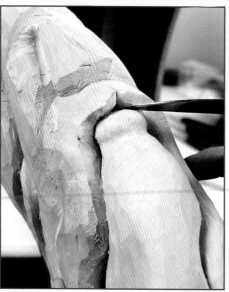

40 Here you can see where the gouge was used. You can also see the separation between the lips.

41 Make a stop cut from the high corner of the nose to the low corner of the nose.

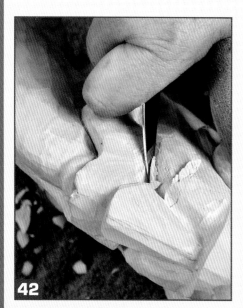

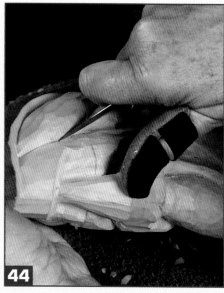

42 Carve the edge of the moustache back toward the face and under the nose.

43 This is what the Knee Spirit should look like at this point. Notice that the moustache overhangs the bottom lip and that you have some roundness to indicate a chin.

44 With a knife, make a stop cut down the hairline.

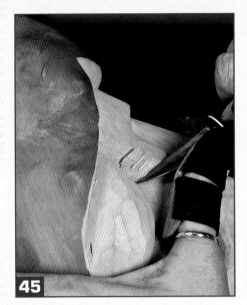

45

When you carve in the temple, use a U-gouge or a knife, whichever you are more comfortable using. The temple should be just outside the eye socket, between the brow bone and the cheekbone. (For more information on this measurement, see part 1 in Figure 2.1 on page 4.)

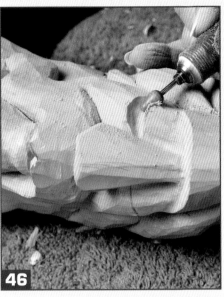

46

Using the pear-shaped bit, carve in deeply on the line you have drawn for the bottom of the eye socket. (For more information on this measurement, see part 3 in Figure 2.1 on page 4.)

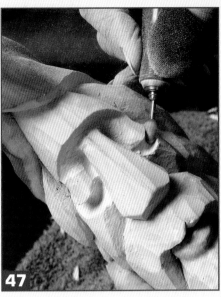

47

Ease up on the depth as you get to the temple because this line should flow right into the temple area.

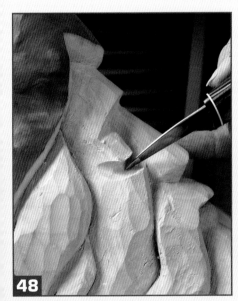

48

The bottom of the eye socket should be deeper than the top. This picture demonstrates that.

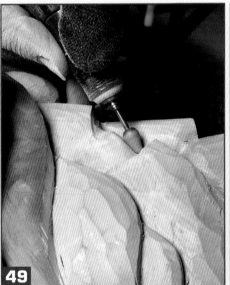

49

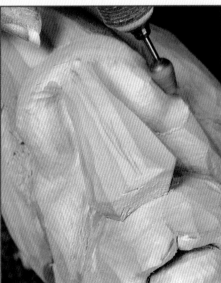

Using the pear-shaped bit, round this area, making sure to keep it deeper at the bottom of the socket. Notice how the line from the eye socket flows right into the temple. This is a good time to study some reference material, so check out your own face in a mirror.

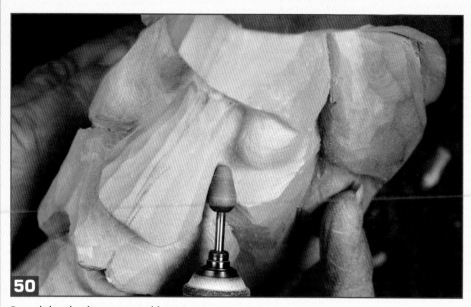

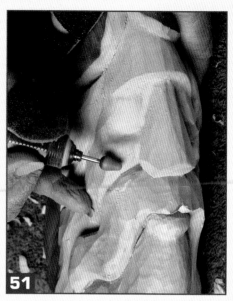

Round the cheek over smoothly.

Be careful not to flatten this area.

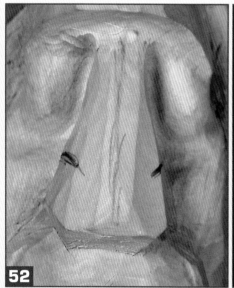

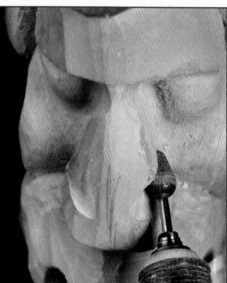

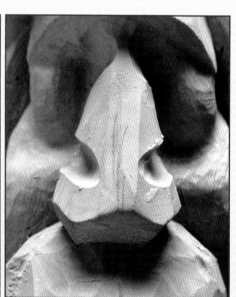

About one-third of the way up the nose, draw a line that follows the line from the high corner of the nose to the low corner. You don't want these lines to meet. Carve these lines with a pear-shaped bit. This is how the carving should look at this point.

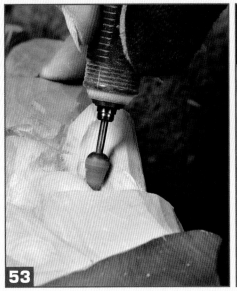
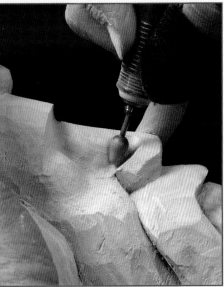

53

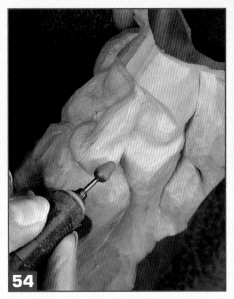

54

Narrow the nose where it meets the forehead. Smooth and shape the sides of the nose.

Round over and smooth the flare of the nose.

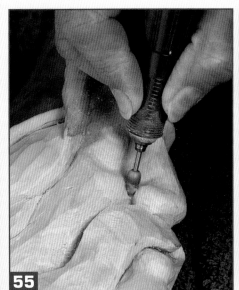

55

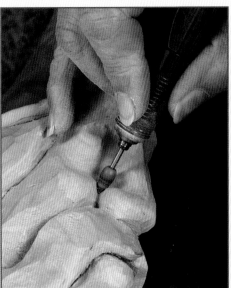
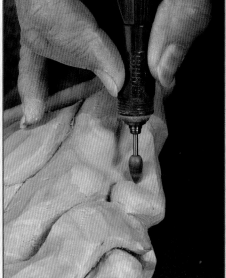

Using a flame- or tear-shaped bit, start at the base of the nose and follow the shape of the flare of the nose until it meets the side of the nose. This gives the nose some definition.

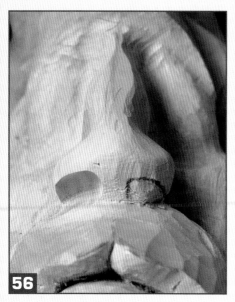

56

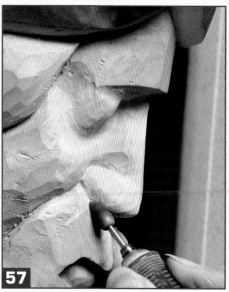

57

Draw the nostrils. They are larger than you think. Check out your own nostrils in a mirror. This photograph shows one side drawn and the other side carved.

Lay the flame-shaped bit on its side against the side of the nose. Push toward the center, not up. Be careful not to carve all the way through the wood to the other nostril.

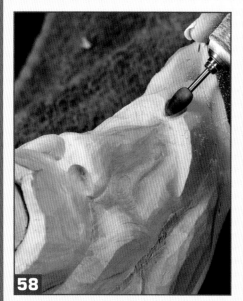

58

59

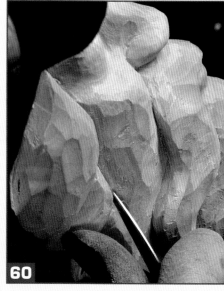

60

Separate the eyebrows using the flame-shaped bit.

Round the hard edge.

With a knife, reinforce the stop cut along the hairline.

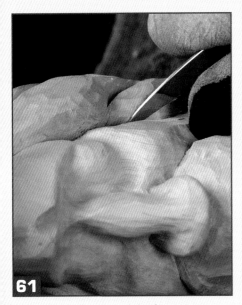

61

Do this on both sides of the face so you have something to carve against when you carve the cheek hollow.

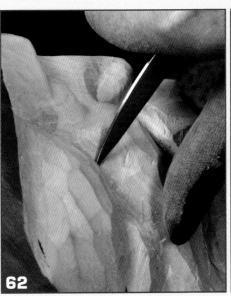

62

The hollows of the cheeks start straight out from the high corner of the nose. You can see that in this picture. (For more information on this measurement, see part 7 in Figure 2.1 on page 4.)

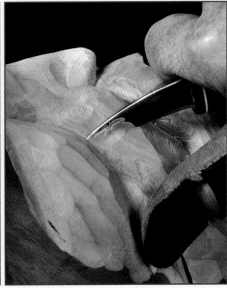

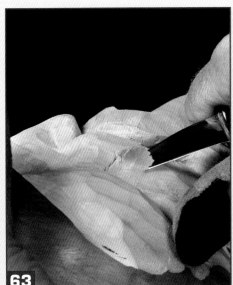

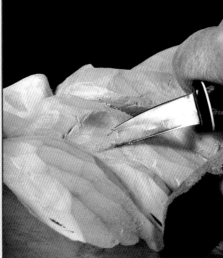

63

Take out a good bit of wood here to emphasize the cheekbones and the cheek hollows.

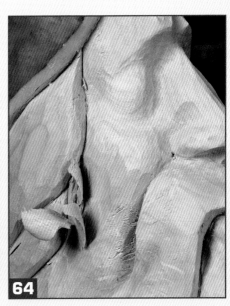

64

This photograph shows you how much wood needs to come out. Notice also the downward slant of the eye socket.

65

You have to take some wood out here to join the back of the cheek and the front of the cheek.

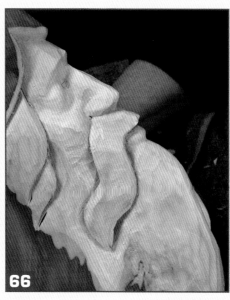

66

This photograph shows the piece at this point.

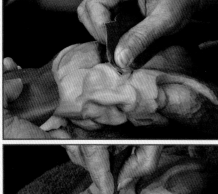

67

Now it's time to sand. You only have to sand the face, but it must be really smooth. Roll cloth-backed sandpaper into a cone shape to get into every little crevice.

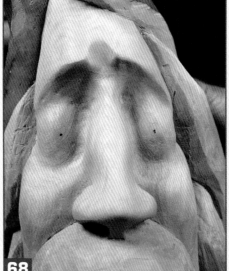

68

Make a small dot in the lower middle of the eye socket with a pencil. Then, using an eye punch, just barely cover the dot and push in lightly. This is not the eye; it's just to let us know where the eye will be.

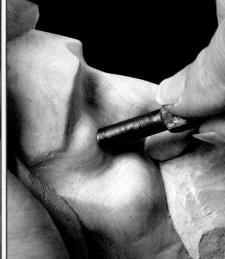

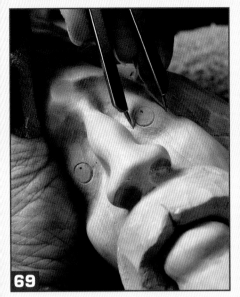

69

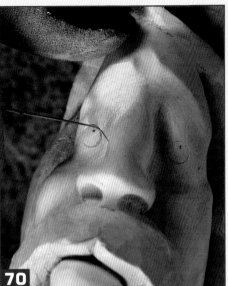

70

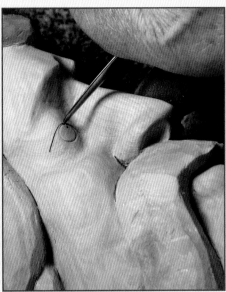

Using dividers, straddle the circle to mark the inside and outside corners of the eye. Mark the inside corner of the eye even with the middle of the eye; mark the outside corner of the eye lower than the middle of the circle. Push in lightly, and then do the other side to match. You have now established the corners of the eyes.

Starting from the dot on the inside corner of the eye, make a stop cut up to the top of the circle. Then starting from the outside dot, stop cut up to the top of the circle to meet the first cut. Now do the same on the other eye.

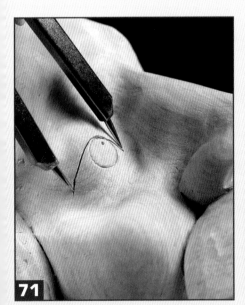

71

72

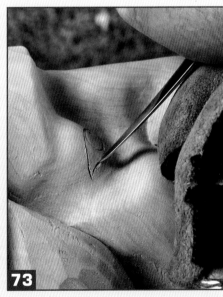

73

Now just to be sure you've got it right, use dividers to measure from one corner of the eye to the other. The measurements of one eye must match the measurements of the other eye.

Now see if you have one eye-width between the eyes. (For more information on this measurement, see part 5 in Figure 2.1 on page 4.) The distance from one corner of the eye to the other corner of the same eye should match the measurement between the eyes.

Make a stop cut from the outside corner of the eye to just under the circle.

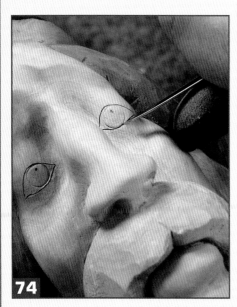

74

Make a stop cut from the inside corner of the eye to meet the first cut under the circle. Do both eyes.

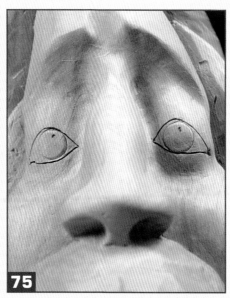

75

This photograph shows how the carving should look now. Remember, the circle is not the pupil, only a guide for the size and placement of the eye.

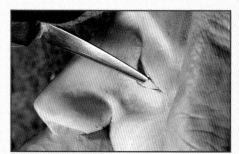

76

Gently lift out the inside and outside corners of both eyes.

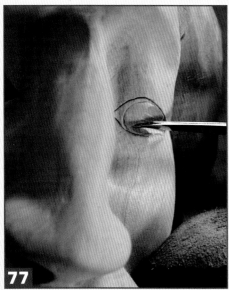

77

Starting from the very top of the eye, carve down to the bottom eyelid. Carve the circle completely away. Take just a sliver of wood out from under the top eyelid.

78

The eyes should look like the ones shown here.

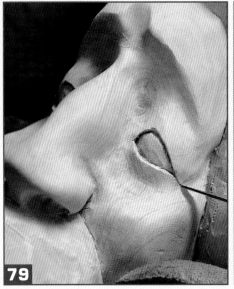

79

80

Extend the cut from the corner of the top eyelid, and then carve back to it to make the fold at the corner of the eye. Do both eyes.

Follow the curve of the eye to make a stop cut for the fold in the eyelid.

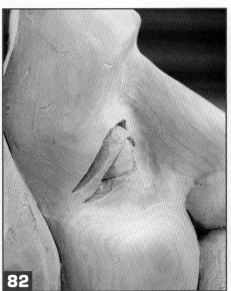
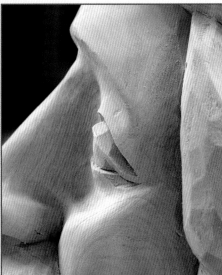

81

82

Carve back to the stop cut rather deeply so that it looks like the eyelid can roll back under the fold.

The eyes should look like the ones shown here.

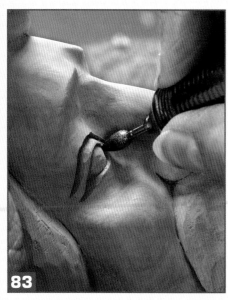
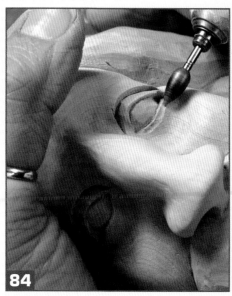
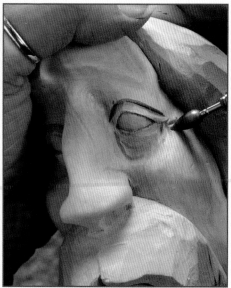

83

Using the flame-shaped bit, just barely push the point of the bit into the inner corners of the eyes to make the tear ducts.

84

Lay the flame-shaped bit on its side and make a small depression just under the eyelash line. Do not try to use the point; it will dig in. Make several lines from each corner of the eye, but don't let them meet. Then carve a few small laugh lines running off those lines at the corners of the eyes. (See Figure 2.6 for guidance on the placement of wrinkles.) Sand smoothly.

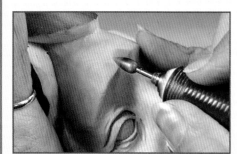
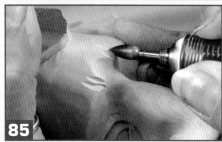
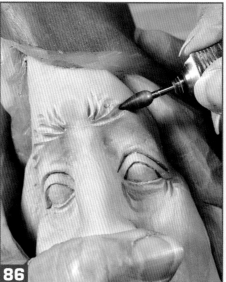
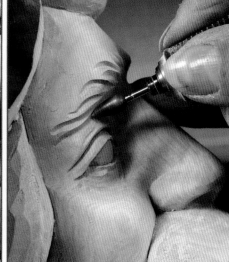

85

On each side of the valley between the eyebrows, use the flame-shaped bit to make two or three wild hairs going straight up.

86

Then, begin to take the lines up and tip them over to the side. The farther you go toward the outside of the face, the more the lines should lie over to the side. Clean out the wood under the last hair so the eyebrow will look raised.

Next, make a few lines all over the hair, moustache, and beard just to get a feel for the flow. I begin under the nose.

Then I move to the inside corner of the mouth. Be sure to keep the bit lying on its side as you pull it through the wood.

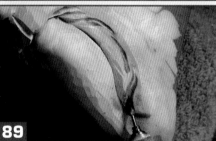

Now continue down the moustache.

Just a few lines here and there will set the flow over the whole piece. Notice that there are no straight lines. They all bend.

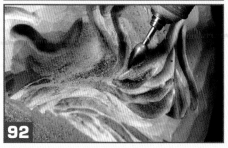

91

Gradually add more and more. Do not start or stop two hairs next to each other in the same place. Always stagger a long hair and a short hair. You can run them alongside each other and into each other, but don't cross them.

92

Make long, flowing lines with a lot of curve to them. Make some very deep lines and some very shallow ones. Add lots of bend and curve. Don't make any straight lines.

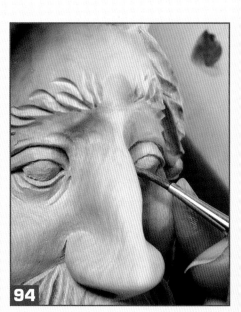

93

I can't stress enough to make long, flowing lines. If the lines are too short, the Knee Spirit will look like he is growing fur. Now sand, sand, sand. Make sure there are no rough spots anywhere on the piece. Make sure the eyes and wrinkles in the face are sanded smooth.

94

Refer back to the painting tips in Chapter Two before you begin to paint. I use acrylic paint for the eyes. Thin the white paint so that it is very thin and cover the whole eye with it. Make sure to keep it off the eyelid. Allow the paint to dry completely before going on to the next step.

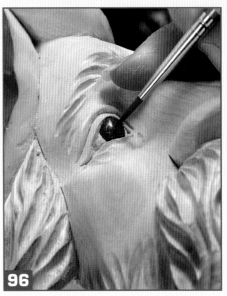

This fellow will have brown eyes, so choose a good, rich brown and paint the irises of the eyes, remembering that part of the iris is under the eyelid. (See Figure 2.3 on page 8.) Dry the paint well with a hair dryer. Do not draw little round balls.

I used a metallic copper for the reflected light. This color will go on the left sides and bottoms of both eyes as you look at the piece. Again, be sure the paint is dry before going on.

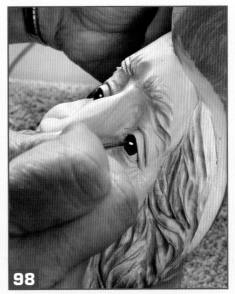

Paint the pupil with black, covering most of the reflected light. Just leave a little crescent of the copper color showing. Allow the paint to dry.

The little white highlight is what really lights the face up, but it must be in the right place. Place this dot in the one o'clock or two o'clock position, partly on the pupil and partly on the iris. Be sure it is completely dry before going on to the next step.

Now we are going to switch to oil paint. Wet down the cheek area with mineral spirits. Keep it out of the high part of the cheek; this is the highlight area. The mineral spirits will keep the paint from grabbing in one spot. Study Figure 2.2 and Figure 2.7 carefully before going on.

100

101

Mix just a little bit of vermilion and just the tiniest bit of burnt sienna with a good bit of mineral spirits. You just want a thin wash. Brush it on in a U shape on the cheeks, staying out of the highlight area. You can use your finger to smudge and blend the color.

Brush some color on the lip, and then blend it with your finger. You don't want a lipline, or the Knee Spirit will appear to be wearing lipstick.

102

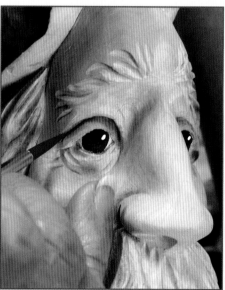

103

Put some color on the insides of the bottom eyelids and in the corners of the eyes. Add a touch of color in all of the little wrinkles. Be sure to put some color in the fold of the eyelids. Brush a little color between the eyebrows.

Don't forget to put some color inside the nostrils.

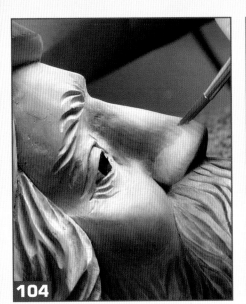

104

105

Put some color down the side of the nose, just to shade it a little bit, and in the crease of the flare of the nose. Add some color just above the ball of the nose. Do not put color on the end of the nose. That is a highlight area.

When the paint is dry, it will be a lighter color. Spray the finished piece lightly with Deft Semi-Gloss clear spray, and just watch what a pretty flesh color the Knee Spirit will turn. Let the finish dry, and then spray the piece one or two more times. Don't forget to sign your finished work.

Carving Father Christmas

I suppose everyone over the age of about eight or ten knows that the stories about all the different Santas are fantasy. Isn't it fun, though, to use your imagination and indulge in fantasy sometimes? Just look at his beard—now that's fantasy!

The hair and beard will be handled differently on this project than on the knee spirit. We'll be burning the hair to get a more realistic look. We will also be carving the entire figure as opposed to only the face.

Materials List

Wood
Cypress knee or wood of choice

Supplies
Pencil and permanent marker
Rotary tool with circular saw bit, a large
    pear-shaped diamond or ruby bit, and a
    flame- or tear-shaped bit
Power chisel
Knife of choice
U-gouge
Cloth-backed sandpaper, 220–400 grit
Eye punch
Dividers
Drum sander with fine sandpaper, xxxx grit
Woodburner with a tight round tip
Paintbrushes: round, sizes #1, #3, and #5
                flat, sizes #2, #4, and #6
Motor oil or linseed oil
Hair dryer
Mineral spirits
Deft semi-gloss clear spray

Acrylic Paints	**Oil Paints**
Metallic gold	Vermilion
Deep green	Burnt sienna
Red	Titanium white
White	Naples yellow
Dark blue	Ivory black
Light blue	Burnt umber
Black	Rose madder

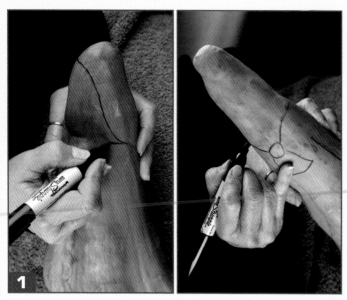

1 After studying the knee to see where I want to put the face, I start to draw. Once I get the pattern laid out in pencil and I'm pleased with what I have, I use a permanent marker to go over the pencil lines so I won't lose the pattern.

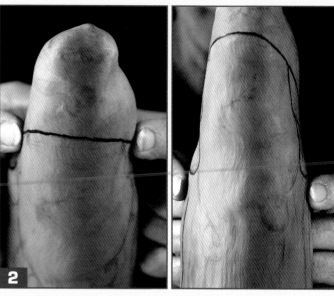

2 Be sure to get the hood even on both sides when you draw the layers of hair. Also make sure that the bottom layers are even across from each other, otherwise the shoulders won't be even.

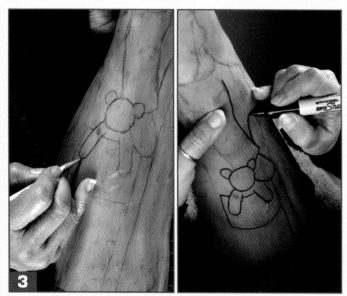

3 This knee has enough bulk to hang Father Christmas's toy bag over one shoulder and put a teddy bear in a pocket on the other side. I think he needs a walking stick too, don't you?

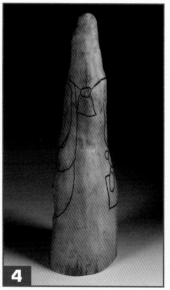

4 Father Christmas is going to have a very long beard and a tassel on the back of his hood. Notice that I have not drawn the face. Try to learn to see the face in your mind. Also, if you use pencil or ink to draw the face, it will smear on the wood and ruin your flesh color.

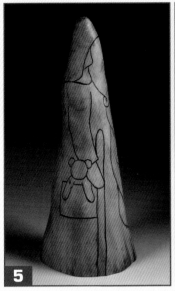
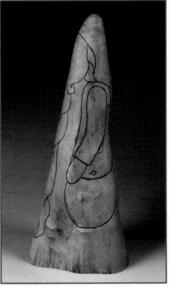

5

I have chosen a knee with an A shape. This shape ensures that I'll have enough width to carve the shoulders.

6

Make a stop cut all the way around the hood and the tassel using the circular saw bit. Don't stop cut the hair yet.

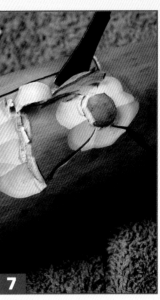

7

Start by carving the knot on the tassel with the power chisel.

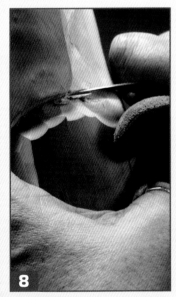

8

Then, using a knife, carve all the way around the hood.

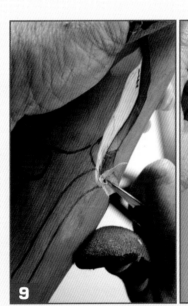
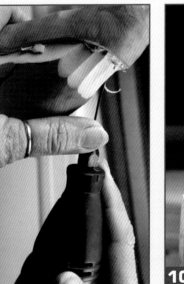

9

You can see here about how deep you should carve around the hood. You can also see that I'm beginning to shape the profile.

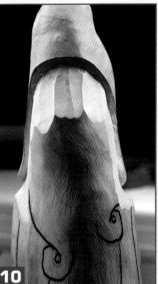

10

You should be able to see the hood on both sides as you look at it from the front. Redraw the layers of hair that were removed as you carved. When you are redrawing, use pencil. Once the skin is removed, the wood will absorb the ink of a marker.

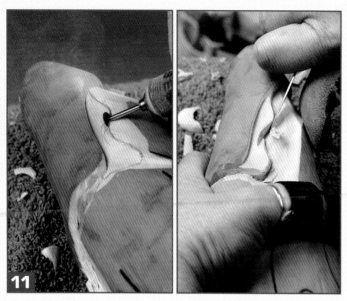

Stop cut the top layer of hair with a circular saw bit and carve it with a knife. Then carve the bottom layer. Carve straight up the side of the hair to start blocking in the face.

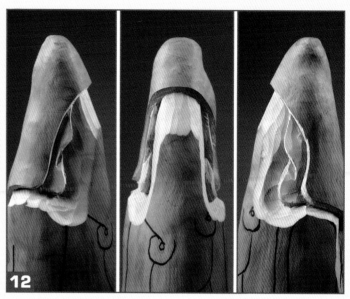

You should be able to see the hair on both sides of the face as you look at it from the front. Carve straight in across the top of the shoulder. As you carve under the bottom layer of hair, start to round over the front part of the shoulder. You can use your power chisel or your knife for this step—choose whichever you are more comfortable using.

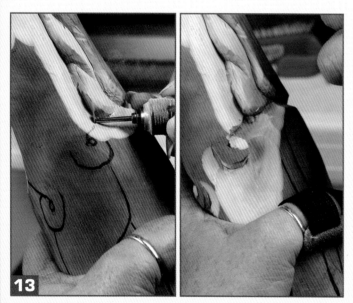

Redraw the beard where you carved it off. You will probably need to move it in closer, under the face. Keep in mind that the beard comes straight down from the face, not way out on the shoulders. As you carve the curls, tuck the tops of them under themselves. These curls will eventually become the ends of the moustache.

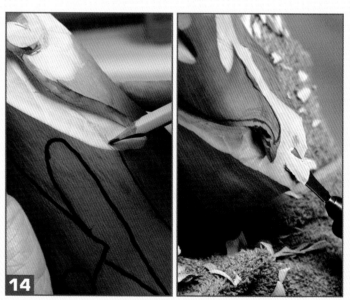

Continue to carve the beard one layer at a time, all the way down to the tip. Be sure to carve deeply so that the beard will lie nice and high on top of his coat.

15

Here you can see how I've carved straight in across the top of the shoulders. It's important to think about this when you are laying out the design. You have to plan for enough width for the shoulders.

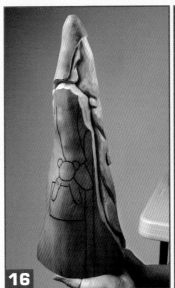
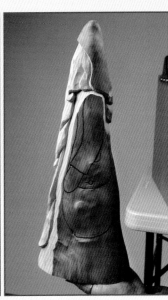

16

Here you can see how deep I've carved into the knee. Notice how I've rounded over the shoulders. This is the beginning of how you will shape the arms.

17

To carve Father Christmas's face, follow Steps 9 through 86 of Chapter Five: Carving a Knee Spirit Step-by-Step. You will follow exactly the same steps, except that between Steps 22 and 23, you will bring the moustache all the way down to meet the curls that you see in Step 13. They will form the ends of the moustache. To finish the piece up, give the face a few wrinkles across the forehead. Your thumbnail should do the job nicely.

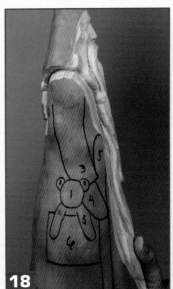
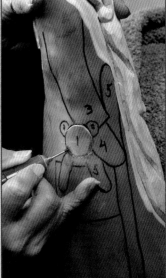

18

Here I've numbered the order in which you'll carve each part. It's just like doing a relief carving. Start by carving the teddy bear's head using the circular saw bit.

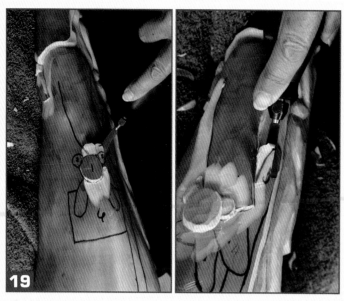

After you carve the head, carve the ears. Next, carve Father Christmas's arm.

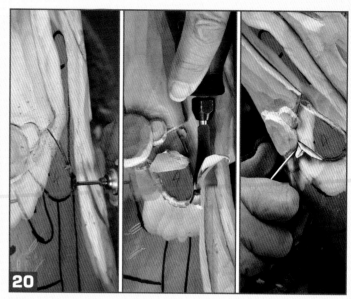

Father Christmas's hand is next. Notice that his hand overlaps the teddy bear's arm. Little things like this make a difference in the appearance of your carving.

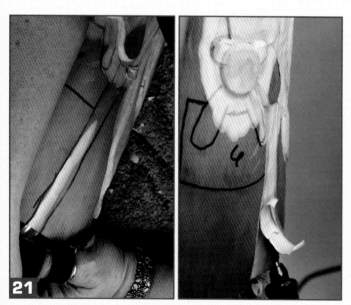
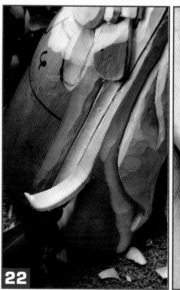

The teddy bear's arm and Father Christmas's walking stick should be at the same depth since his hand overlaps them both.

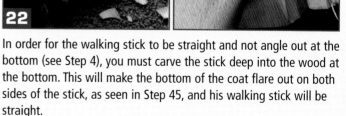

In order for the walking stick to be straight and not angle out at the bottom (see Step 4), you must carve the stick deep into the wood at the bottom. This will make the bottom of the coat flare out on both sides of the stick, as seen in Step 45, and his walking stick will be straight.

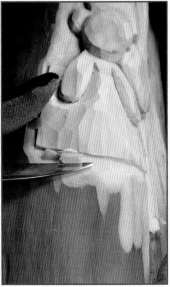

23 Now carve the pocket.

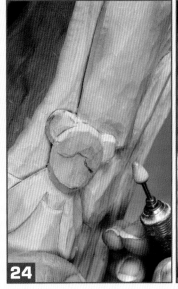
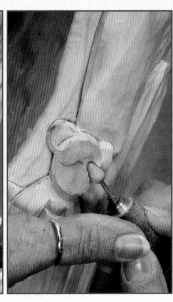

24 Here you can see how I've drawn the teddy bear's nose. Lay your pear-shaped bit on its side and carve a groove above that line.

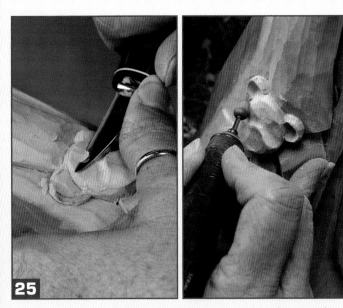

25 Then carve away everything above that groove. Round over and smooth the area. Hollow out the ears.

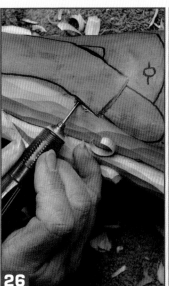

26 Using the circular saw bit, stop cut around the sleeve on the other side, and use the power chisel to carve in deep around the sleeve. Then, carve the hand.

27

At the top of the shoulder, carve straight in under the strap that goes to the toy bag. The strap lies on top of the shoulder. Carve deeply down the side of the arm, especially in the bend of the arm.

28

Carve deeply under the bottom of the bag but not too deeply under the flap of the bag.

29

Carve all of the skin off. If you have any interesting little ripples, leave that area intact, but be sure when you sand that you blend that part into the rest so you won't have a set line that will show when you paint. (See the project on page 38 in the Gallery and notice how the skin in the back blends in with the rest of the carving.)

30

There are many different ways to sand. If you carve clean (which means that you have left no fuzzies) and you don't want to sand, then don't. I personally like the look and feel of the piece when it's sanded smooth.

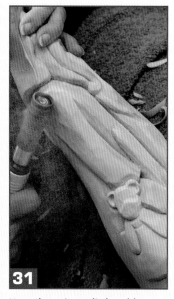

31

Here I'm using a little rubber-covered drum sander that is covered with fine sandpaper. It does a nice job, but there is still a lot of hand sanding to do. Sometimes I use a flap wheel.

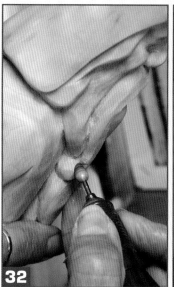

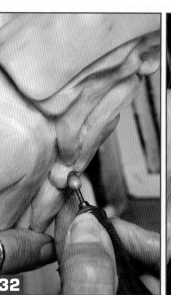

32

Now it's time to get ready to burn the beard. I start by hollowing out the middle of the curls. I draw my flame-shaped bit down under the nose to make a little depression in the moustache and make another depression where the moustache leaves the corner of the mouth.

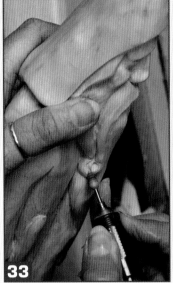

33

Where I've hollowed out the middle of the curls, I lay my flame-shaped bit on its side and pull up from the curl following the shape of the moustache.

34

Make a few lines down from the moustache. Hair always grows down first (except for eyebrows). Once you have moved a little way out from the face, you can begin to twist and curl the hair. Make a few breaks in the hair. Start down first on every layer of hair.

35

Remember, no straight lines. Even straight hair bends. Make just a few long, curving lines.

36

You don't want to make too many lines here because we are going to burn the hair on this piece.

37

Study this picture to give you an idea of how many lines to carve. Generally speaking, you'll need just enough to break the hair up.

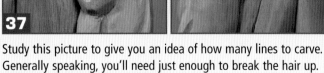

38 Here you can see the overall breaks I have made in the hair and beard. If you don't want to burn the beard, go ahead and continue to carve the whole beard. Just remember, make long, flowing lines.

39 Using a tight round tip, I begin the burning process by making guidelines all over the beard and hair. This gives me the feel for the flow. You want to make sure all your lines bend and flow smoothly *away* from and *into* each other. You never want to cross one line with another because this can cause breakage.

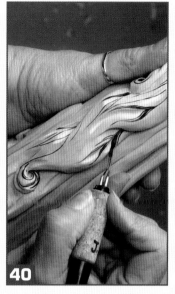

40 Notice that where I've carved the breaks in the beard, I make a part there by burning *away* from the break to each side of the break and let that flow right *into* the next break.

41 Gradually let the lines flow back alongside of and into each other. Keep all your lines long and flowing. I use a tight round tip on my burner for most everything.

42 Here you can see the overall flow of Father Christmas's great, long beard. Now that you have developed the direction the hair will fall, go back and fill it all in. Stagger the length of the hairs, but make them all long and flowing (see Figure 2.8 on page 10).

43 Don't forget to burn in the face of the teddy bear. As you can see from the photograph, I use very simple lines for this.

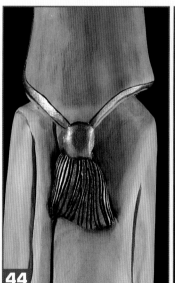

44 As you are burning the hair, keep in mind how fine hair is. Make your lines as close together as you can. On the other hand, when you are burning in the strings for the tassel, make them wider apart than the lines for the hair because the strings are much thicker than the hair.

45

46

47

Here you can see the teddy bear's face. I burned a border around Father Christmas's hood and sleeves and added some holly leaves. Once the burning is finished, we're ready to paint. When I want something to be opaque, I use acrylic paint, and everything acrylic paint is used on has to be done first, before going on to oil paints. I began by painting the gold trim.

I also use acrylic paint for the tassel. When you are painting the tassel, paint across the burn. You want the burn to show between each string. Choose a pretty, soft gold metallic for this.

Here I'm using a deep green acrylic paint for the leaves and for the rim inside the gold trim. Later, we'll paint some bright red berries between the leaves.

48

49

50

Next, I paint the hood with motor oil. Let it soak up as much as it will, then wipe it off and do it again, until it won't soak up any more. You can use linseed oil if you prefer it to motor oil; I just don't like the smell. The motor oil or the linseed oil lets the natural color of the skin show.

Paint the eyes with acrylic paint. Thin white paint and paint the whole eyeball. Try to keep it off the eyelids. Allow the paint to dry. (Refer to the Painting Blue Eyes section on page 7 for more information.)

Paint the whole iris a nice, dark blue. Remember, no little round balls. Part of the iris is under the eyelid (see Figure 2.3 on page 8).

51

52

53

Put some light blue on the left side of each eye, staying inside of the dark blue. Allow the paint to dry, and then paint the pupil black (see Figures 2.4 and 2.5 on page 8).

Just one tiny little dot of white paint in the one o'clock or two o'clock position of the pupil will make Father Christmas look wide-awake and alert (see Figure 2.6 on page 8). Now put your acrylic paints away.

Wet the cheeks with mineral spirits, making sure to stay out of the high part of his cheeks since this is the highlight area and should not get any color (see Figure 2.2 on page 6 and Figure 2.7 on page 9).

54

55

Mix a little vermilion and a tiny bit of burnt sienna with mineral spirits. Thin this mix like a wash. *Lightly* brush this on Father Christmas's cheeks in a U shape and blend it with your finger. Brush a little of this mix on the lips.

Put a little of the same color mix in the eyelid creases and in all the wrinkles. Be careful not to have too much color on your brush. You can always add more color, but it's hard to take off.

Put just a little color down the sides of the nose and between the eyebrows. Do this cautiously—too little is better than too much.

Don't forget to add color to the forehead wrinkles and inside the nostrils.

I mix titanium white, a tiny amount of Naples yellow, and just a smidge of ivory black for the hair and beard. Using a dry brush with very little paint, I paint across the burn lines.

Continue to dry brush this color until you've covered all the hair. There are some spots where you will have to paint with the burn, but be careful to use only a small amount of paint. You don't want to fill up the burn lines.

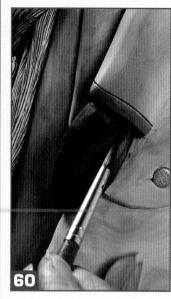

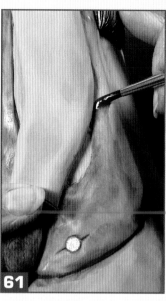

60 Use burnt umber, thinned with mineral spirits and mixed with a little motor oil, for Father Christmas's mittens.

61 For Father Christmas's bag, the teddy bear, and the walking stick, use several coats of motor oil for a rich honey color.

62 There are many beautiful colors of red that you can use for Father Christmas's coat, or you can mix your own. For this piece, I chose rose madder. Mix a couple of finger length strings out of the tube with three or four times that much mineral spirits (sometimes more) and a couple of tablespoonfuls of motor oil. You want it to be thin—it is just a wash.

63 Paint the hard-to-reach, closed-in areas first: between the bag and the beard, the sleeves, around the beard and around the bag.

64 If the area starts to look splotchy, give it another coat of paint while it is still wet, and maybe even a third coat.

65 Painting between the beard and the walking stick is easier to do before the back is painted so that you can hold on to the piece.

66 Dry the paint with a hair dryer for 1 to 15 minutes. Then let the piece co for another 10 to 15 minutes. The paint will still be tacky to the touch Next, spray the carving lightly with several coats of Deft semi-gloss spray. If you have time, let the piece dry overnight and then spray it with Deft. Once you've sprayed the piece do not dry it with the hair dryer because the paint will bubble. Now didn't he come out grand?

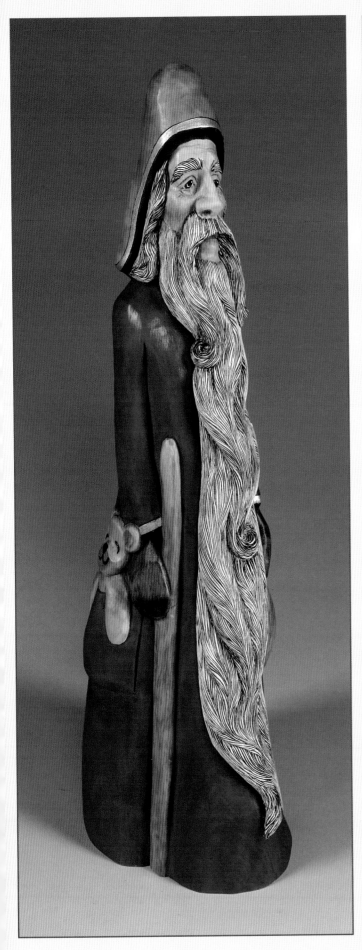

Carving an Elf

T here are stories about elves from all over the world. Some tales tell of elves that are good and kind and some tell of elves with very bad tempera- ments. Because he is fantasy being, you can make this elf whatever you want. My elves are always good and kind and maybe a little mischievous. Elves' ears are so big that you can't hide them under their hats, and when you see them, you know immediately that they're elves. Most elves look like they know a secret that they won't share.

Again, this project gives you a chance to practice your face-carving skills.

Materials List

Wood
Cypress knee or wood of choice

Supplies
Pencil and permanent marker
Rotary tool with circular saw bit, a large
    pear-shaped diamond or ruby bit, and a
    flame- or tear-shaped bit
Power chisel
Knife of choice
U-gouge
Cloth-backed sandpaper, 220–400 grit
Eye punch
Dividers
Woodburner with a tight round tip
Paintbrushes: round, sizes #1, #3, and #5
                flat, sizes #2, #4, and #6
Motor oil or linseed oil
Hair dryer
Mineral spirits
Deft semi-gloss clear spray
Steel wool, #0000

Acrylic Paints   **Oil Paints**
White   Vermilion
Dark green   Burnt sienna
Metallic gold
Black

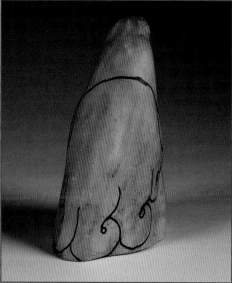
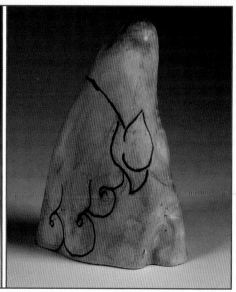

Draw the ears, hair, beard, and hat with a pencil and then with a permanent marker. The ears are most important. Make sure they are even on both sides. You can really play with the beard, making curls or making it long and scraggly. Just have fun with him.

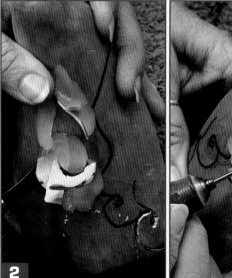
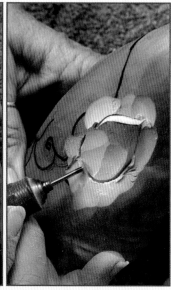

Stop cut around the ears. Carve away the wood around the ears. Then carve off the bottom of the ears. Stop cut around the bottom again, and then carve the wood around them away again so the bottom of the ears will be close to the head.

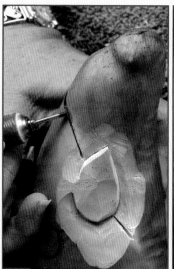

Make a stop cut around the bottom of the hat. Don't go all the way around. We'll leave the back intact to show off the ripples of the knee. Carve away the wood under the hat.

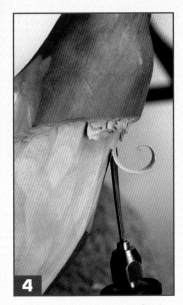
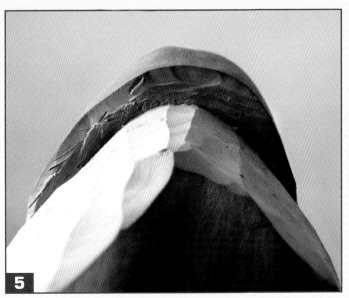
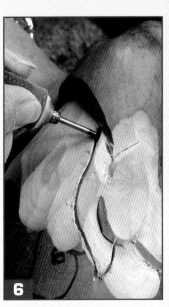

Begin to establish the profile by carving from where the end of the nose will be to the hat. Take very little off at the end of the nose, but get deeper and deeper as you get to the hat.

This is the beginning of the shape of the nose as you look at it from the bottom up.

Stop cut the hair and remove a lot of wood around the hair.

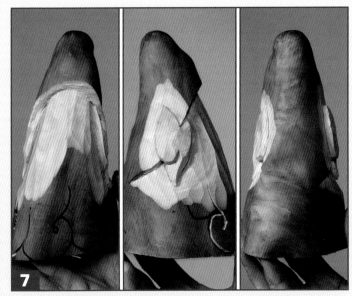

Carve straight up along the hairline to shape the side of the face. As you look at it from the front, you should be able to see the hair on each side of the face. From the back you can see the ears.

Stop cut the curls around the beard. As you carve, pay attention to which curls overlap the next. Carve deeply around each one so they stand on their own.

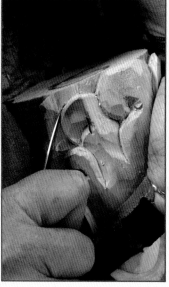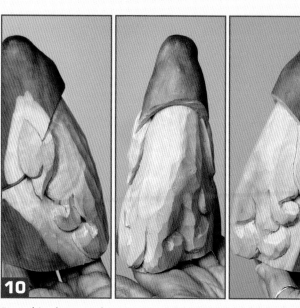

Continue to carve in layers so that each curl shows at a different depth.

From this photograph, you can see how deep you need to carve in order for each curl to show.

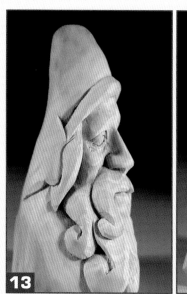

Now carve the fur band on his hat.

Make sure the fur band stands up nice and high so that when you nick it to create the fur, the band will show nicely.

To carve the face, follow the instructions for Step 9 through Step 84 in Chapter Five: Carving a Knee Spirit Step-by-Step. Please read the Painting Tips, pages 5 to 10, before going on to paint.

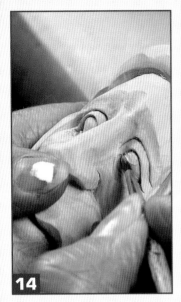

14

Thin white acrylic paint (I usually use my thumbnail for my palette because it's convenient) and paint the whole eyeballs of both eyes, being very careful not to get paint on the eyelids. Dry well before going on to the next step (see the Painting Blue Eyes sidebar on page 7 for more information).

15

This fellow will have green eyes, so choose a rich, dark green and paint the irises (see Figures 2.3 to 2.6 on page 8 and the eye color chart on page 7). Dry well.

16

Using metallic gold paint, put some on the left side and bottom of both eyes. Be sure to keep the paint inside the green iris. Dry well. Then, paint the pupil, painting right over the gold to leave just a thin crescent of gold showing (see Figures 2.4 and 2.5 on page 8).

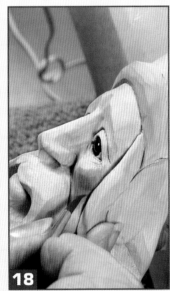
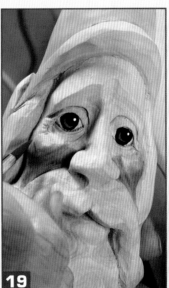
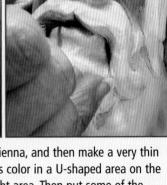

17

Put just a small white dot in the one o'clock or two o'clock position of the pupils, partly on the black and partly on the green (see Figure 2.6 on page 8). This really wakes the elf up. Dry well and put the acrylic paints away.

18

From now on we'll be using oil paint. Wet the cheeks with mineral spirits, making sure to stay out of the highlight areas of the cheeks (see Figure 2.2 on page 6 and Figure 2.7 on page 9).

19

Mix vermilion and a little burnt sienna, and then make a very thin wash with mineral spirits. Put this color in a U-shaped area on the cheeks, staying out of the highlight area. Then put some of the same color on his lips, making sure to avoid creating a lip line. Blend the color with your finger.

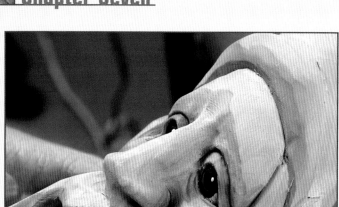

20

Put some color in the creases of the eyelids and in all of the little wrinkles.

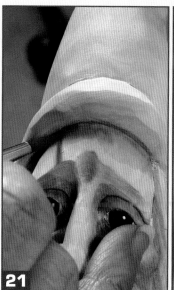

21

Put some color along the hat line, and then blend it very quickly with your finger.

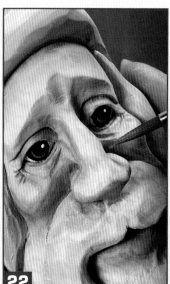

22

Now add some color down the side of the nose and in the flare of the nose. Put just a little across the bridge of the nose, but not on the end of the nose.

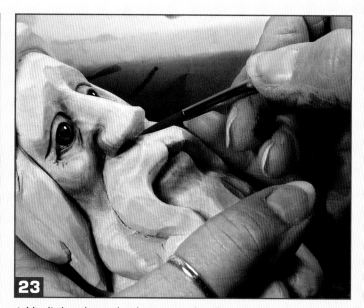

23

Add a little color under the nose and in the nostrils. Dry well.

To burn the hair and beard, follow Steps 39 to 42 and 44 in Chapter Six: Carving Father Christmas Step-by-Step.

24

Now paint the hat, the shoulders, and the back with motor oil. Let the piece set for 15 minutes, and then wipe it off with a soft cloth. Repeat this process until the wood stops soaking up the oil. Do not put motor oil on the face or the beard. Spray the piece lightly (even though the motor oil is not completely dry) with several coats of Deft Semi-Gloss. Allow it to dry between coats. If the finish gets too shiny, I rub it down with very fine steel wool once it is completely dry then vacuum to get all the little particles out. Now isn't he just too cute?

Resources

Cypress Knees, Seminars, and Basswood Blanks for this Father Christmas

Carole Jean Boyd is available to teach seminars on carving cypress knees at clubs and schools. She also sells cypress knees that she has personally selected and has drawn patterns on. For more information, contact her at:

4641 Warren Drive
Millbrook, AL 36054
(334) 868-9999

Cypress Knees
Louisiana Cypress Products
217 Sterns Road
Olla, LA 71465
(318) 495-5450
Fax: (318) 495-5727
cen41581@centurytel.net
www.cypressknee.com

Colwood Electronics
(732) 938–5556
www.woodburning.com
woodburning tools and supplies

Ryobi Tools
www.ryobitools.com
power carving tools

Smoky Mountain Woodcarvers Supply
1–800–541–5994
www. woodcarvers.com
woodcarving tools and supplies

The Tool Box
(432) 553–5996
www.thecarverstoolbox.com
woodcarving tools and supplies

The Woodcraft Shop
1–800–397–2278
www.thewoodcraftshop.com
woodcarving tools and supplies

For more resources, visit **www.FoxChapelPublishing.com** and click "Resources."

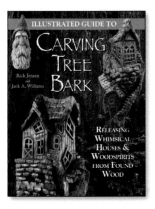

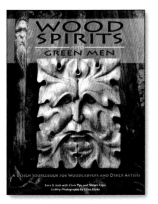

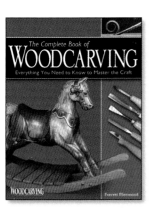

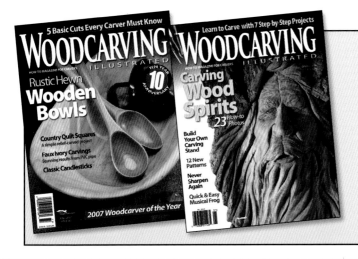